THE FORTUNES OF CYNICUS

VICTORIAN CARTOONIST AND POSTCARD DESIGNER

Cynicus
(Martin Anderson)
about 1902

The FORTUNES
of CYNICUS

VICTORIAN CARTOONIST AND POSTCARD DESIGNER

ELSPETH REID and FLORA DAVIDSON

TEMPORA MUTANTUR.

FOREST LODGE

Published by Forest Lodge
Dykehead
By Kirriemuir
Scotland DD8 4QN

Pictures from the authors' collection

ISBN 0-9525979-0-X

British Library cataloguing-in-print data has been
applied for

Typeset in New Century 10/12pt by Scriptmate Editions
Manufacture coordinated in UK by Book-in-Hand Ltd
20 Shepherds Hill, London N6 5AH

CONTENTS

In Memoriam
John (Ian) Davidson,
who started us off

Acknowledgements

We wish to record our special debt to Wilfrid B Grubb of Edinburgh, the expert on Cynicus postcards, who made his knowledge and collection freely available. We are grateful for the materials provided by Bob Allan of Cupar, and information from James MacGregor MBE of Dunfermline and George Hepburn of Strathkinness, all of whom died while the book was in progress; to D Wilkie Gahan, Broughty Ferry, for the gift of his father's sketch of Cynicus; Joan Thomson, Broadstairs, for printing blocks; Anne Duckworth, Balmullo, for reminiscences; Philip Paterson, John Synnot of Broughty Ferry, Ian Lindsay of Newport-on-Tay and J Howard Smith of Felpham for access to their collections; G G Bannerman, London, for research at the Public Record Office; Dr Peter Stewart of Hamilton and Walter Cairns of the Scottish Arts Council for their help; Dundee, Southend and Cupar Libraries; St Andrews University Library; Colindale Newspaper Library; the National Library of Scotland; the British Library; the Mitchell Library, Glasgow; Edinburgh Central Library; the Scottish Record Office; the Public Record Office; Surrey Record Office; the Royal Scottish Academy and McManus Galleries, Dundee. We thank North East Fife District Museum Service for providing access to the Cynicus collection and for permission to reproduce copyright photographs; and finally we thank the Reverend W F Ward, of the Church of Saint Mary the Virgin, Arbroath, for his skill and patience with word processing.

Introduction

CYNICUS, MARTIN ANDERSON (1854-1932), has two claims to fame. First, as a total outsider from Scotland he took London by storm in the early 1890s with his satirical cartoons. After that vogue passed he reappeared in Fife as a successful publisher and designer of the first humorous postcards. Such a seemingly simple thing as a comic postcard turns out to be the product of a complex character and have a complicated history.

In 1930 the *Glasgow Evening News* published his memoirs in instalments. They are a mixture of frankness and vagueness, tell only the sunny side of the story and obscure or omit his failures and failings. 'I have ever been a devoted follower of truth', he said, but his emblem was 'Truth' below a lyre. Sixty years after his death, with his personal papers and belongings dispersed or destroyed, getting at the truth takes digging. Almost every published mention of him contains mistakes. This biography clears up some mysteries. We hope we have opened the way for further discoveries.

TRVTH

Fame lightly lends her laurel crown,
Her titles, rank, and dignity

'Tis only when a man is down
She shows her true malignity

Chapter 1—A Rural Childhood 1854–68

'ALL THE TALENTS I ever possessed I owe to her,' said Martin Anderson of his mother. 'She was indeed a remarkable woman, who kept in touch with current literature and events, and besides bringing up and educating her seven children and superintending all our father's business transactions, her knowledge of the classics, ancient and modern, was deep and profound.' It was his mother who insisted on art lessons, music lessons, a study of English literature. She reminded her children of their successful ancestors and incited emulation. Even after death she imposed her will upon them. There were disagreements, as there are in all families, regroupings, reconciliations, and one bitter quarrel that was never forgiven, but on the whole her offspring worked together for most of their lives to realise her hopes for her favourite son, Martin.

She was born Margaret Martin in 1817, in the village of Tayport in Fife, one of two sisters who helped in a ladylike way in the parental drapery business. In that restricted milieu they were too intelligent, too well read, and perhaps too plain to attract husbands. So when Margaret was thirty and presumed to be on the shelf—and unexpectedly had a suitor—she did not hesitate to snap him up. William Anderson was ten years her senior, and occupied a modest position locally, but he came of a respectable Fife family and, we have reason to believe, was handsome and charming. Margaret's father was not charmed. He gave her sixty pounds as a dowry and put a clause in his will excluding her husband from any rights over her inheritance.

Since both their fathers were shareholders in the Edinburgh, Perth and Dundee Railway Company, and the better railway jobs were reserved for shareholders' families, William was provided with a post as stationkeeper at Kingskettle in Fife. In 1847 the couple was married. Life as Mrs Anderson was not quite as Margaret had expected. She made the disagreeable acquaintance of housework and cooking. Moreover, she was immediately, and repeatedly, pregnant. In the first three years she gave birth three times; in all she had nine infants in quick succession, of whom seven survived. Her parents took the first baby off her hands.

It is hard to see how she managed to keep her cultural interests alive, between the constant claims of her babies and the formal demands of Victorian social life. The intellectual Margaret may not have been much of a homemaker. If we can judge from Cynicus's lifelong indifference to comfort and good living, she brought up the family on high thinking and plain fare. The marital disappointment may have been mutual.

After a year or two William was promoted to Leuchars Junction and moved his family to a six-roomed house in the village. In his memoirs Cynicus devotes few words to his father. Clearly Father lacked those characteristics Cynicus so esteemed in Mother: she even had to 'superintend all our father's business transactions'. Cynicus did briefly recall the jaunty figure on Leuchars platform: 'No uniforms were worn, and I can still see my father in his light suit and straw hat. The station-master at Cupar used to march about in top-boots and keep the passengers in order with his riding-whip. The trains were very few and the stations were only opened at train time.' William Anderson's duties therefore left him a good deal of free time, the enjoyment of some dignity, and a free house, but a salary of seventy pounds a year was hardly enough to keep the growing family in style.

Martin, the sixth child and future Cynicus, was born in the village of Leuchars in 1854. Leuchars lies only a mile away from the cold North Sea that sends chill mists and bitter winds across what were then sandy wastes. The hamlet was a huddle of stone cottages with roofs of thatch and red pantiles, clustered round a knoll with a Norman church and the village school that Martin attended. According to him, the schoolchildren dug up bones in the playground and bartered them for candy when the rag and bone man came. The bones were from early Christian graves,

THE PURSUIT OF PLEASURE UNDER DIFFICULTIES

but for Cynicus the 'little hands' were 'diligently excavating the bones of their forefathers to be exchanged for the luscious succulent'.

He was also, revealingly, fond of telling how he and his little friends were caught in a thunderstorm. As they sheltered quaking with terror he told them he knew how to stop thunder, kneeled down before them and recited the only prayer he knew. The thunder ceased. The audience was amazed at his supposed power over Nature. He was amazed at his power over the audience. It was a useful discovery.

When the Andersons left the station house Martin was approaching ten, too young to ponder why his father was no longer employed by the railway company. When they moved from Leuchars to the nearby hamlet of Guardbridge he merely considered it 'a delightful change'. Guardbridge is situated where the River Eden and the Moutray Burn debouch into an estuary. It was a depressing little place at low tide when its expanse of mudflats was uncovered, but at high tide the smallest coasters could come up and subside into the mud to discharge cargo. A branch railway line passed through on its way from Leuchars, carrying golfers and students to nearby St Andrews. There was a minute station, and a siding for the distillery, but William Anderson was not to be seen strolling along the platform in his light suit and straw hat. Instead he would now be pacing the quay in the guise of 'a shipper in a small way'. As his son reported, 'He chartered small vessels from Newcastle and Sunderland with English coal, the returning freights being potatoes and corn from the farms round about, and I have seen four vessels in at one time.' The sudden transition from railway employee to self-employed businessman remains unexplained.

The boys adored playing about the ships' holds and lending a hand. Cynicus had another story about bones with which he liked to make his guests' flesh creep. 'A vessel came from the Black Sea with bone manure for the farmers. On opening one of the bags I noticed small pieces of red and blue cloth with brass buttons which were of British regiments which had been at the Crimea. Reparations with a vengeance.' (The number of buttons had grown with repetition of the story.)

For the children the Eden estuary and Tentsmuir, the wilderness to the north of it, were a paradise. They had a boat and went fishing in the landlocked waters. On Tentsmuir, instead of today's vast conifer plantations and military aerodrome there were miles of gorse and heather fringed with sandy beach all the way to the River Tay. They chased butterflies and caught beetles, and made forts among the sand dunes. It was a period they would sometimes look back on with longing in their Glasgow and London years. Cynicus confessed to a childish stratagem on that shore:

How can I forget a dear old lady, Miss Anderson, an old family friend, who came to stay with us? Being troubled with rheumatism in her ankles, she had been advised to wade in sea water. I used to accompany her for a wicked purpose. With my little spade I dug certain deep holes in the sand at low water, and when they were covered by the rising tide I led her towards them, when she would suddenly topple into one of them with a scream, when I gallantly rescued her from a watery grave and received a whole shilling for my bravery. I think she got suspicious latterly.

As so often when the memoirs recount a seemingly casual anecdote, consciously or unconsciously behind it stands something of greater significance. Miss Anderson was to be important to the family beyond the context of this tale.

In official documents William Anderson is variously described as a coal merchant and a commission agent. These descriptions apply to his shipping venture; it seems to have been a brief interlude, and future events indicate it was not a success. While he continued his experiment in independence his wife was trying to maintain the family's social status. It was hard to keep up appearances with the aid of one maid-of-all-work to repair the ravages of a houseful of children. Willie, Annie, Lizzie, Martin, Nelly and John created an atmosphere of disorder. Discipline had to be strict, the hand of an exasperated mother had to sting.

Then the children would run to Belle, the general servant, nurse and mainstay. Stout Belle Tullis! Plump and smiling, holding out welcoming arms, she is a familiar figure in the work of Cynicus. Once when he and his younger brother dug themselves a cave in the sand dunes it collapsed on them, and darkness fell before they extricated themselves and made for home. It was Belle who led the search party. Where was mother?

Mrs Anderson always welcomed literary visitors. The Cuppleses, novelists and story writers who came to stay nearby, attracted distinguished guests, such as George Macdonald. Martin remembered accompanying Mrs Oliphant to St Andrews to visit the Blackwood publishing family. In his recollection it was to him the Portuguese baron from Earlshall came to teach Spanish and Portuguese; more probably, it was to brother Willie, who eventually became a professional linguist. Martin's ego appropriated the honour.

Like Willie before him, Martin was sent to Madras College, the St Andrews grammar school, travelling daily by train from Guardbridge. Coming home was complicated.

Golf had a much greater attraction for me than the College curriculum. Immediately after school hours I made for the station then situated close to the golf course...and pitching my books into the guard's van and taking out my golf clubs which I kept there I made for the links. Later I might have been seen sitting on the railway fence fully a mile from the station holding up a golf club as the train approached and clambering into the van as it slowed down and being scolded by the genial old guard. I wonder what would happen if this were attempted nowadays at St Andrews. There was just one small engine that plied the branch line and it hauled three carriages for 1st, 2nd, and 3rd class passengers, with a guard's van in the rear. The working staff consisted of the guard, the engine-driver, and the fireman—all St Andrews men.

This happy childhood memory provided the prototype for the most popular of all Cynicus's postcard designs, 'Our Local Express'. Designed about 1903 the card harks back to that bygone age and its leisurely pace of life. (The useful line from Leuchars to St Andrews was closed in the 1960s and Guardbridge station has become a green lawn.)

Cynicus readily admitted to being an indifferent scholar, and it is likely he was the kind of effervescent witty schoolboy that laughs at authority and only gets down to work the day before the exam, with poor results; but he obviously had one talent. To quote J A Hammerton's *Humorists of the Pencil*: 'One who was at school with him tells me that from earliest boyhood [in Leuchars?] Martin Anderson loved to draw caricatures, his slate being

HOME, SWEET HOME.

Be it *ever* so humble, there's no place like home.

more often filled with comic portraits of the teacher and his playmates than the lawful pencillings of the diligent scholar.' Martin himself said:

> A blind man could scarcely have avoided observing the fact that there was one particular direction in which I had a bent, and as there was a total lack of similar indication along the more usual and more profitable lines, my parents and teachers had the good sense to see that I was wasting my time. It was then decided to send me to an art school in Glasgow.

In this easy fashion Cynicus glosses over what was a major upheaval in his family. Margaret must have come to the end of her patience. The family was never going to have a decent income.

Though she did her best to 'superintend' them, her husband's financial experiments were a disaster. Yet that alone would not have forced her to risk scandal and part from him. Dealing with farmers, whether arranging rail transport to market for their beasts or shipping their potatoes, traditionally required every agreement to be sealed with a dram. Since the distillery workers got a free allowance there was plenty of fiery spirit available round about Guardbridge. Had Anderson succumbed to the Scotch disease? Did he embarrass the genteel visitors, noisily rebel against his spouse's commands, or drink his profits? The family were silent about father and never alluded to any such problem. Yet it would explain why they so wholeheartedly rallied round Margaret.

A Family Break-up

Whatever the reason, Margaret wanted to see all her children secure. She confided in old Miss Anderson, who was no relation but the guest young Martin had led into the sea. Miss Anderson approached her brother James, a starch manufacturer in Glasgow, and obtained a place as a commercial clerk for Margaret's eldest boy, Willie. He went to lodge with Margaret's cousin there. Lizzie was sent to join her aunt and eldest sister in Tayport, where she spent the rest of her life in the drapery store. Annie was despatched to an aunt in Perth to train as a teacher. Mrs Anderson then took the three youngest children, Martin, Nelly and John, to the vicinity of Glasgow.

All the signs are that family and friends came to her aid at a critical time. Whatever split the Anderson family conversely showed the strong bonds on the maternal side of it. This closeness of the whole extended tribe, evident time and again, was to help Cynicus over many a rough patch.

Mrs Anderson rented a flat in Rosebank Place, Cambuslang, not too distant from the mansion of Miss Anderson and her brother. Depending on which parent they resembled, some of the Anderson children were plain and some were good-looking; all were undersized. Martin had grown into an extremely handsome youth, dark-haired and bright-eyed.

His person was so small and slight that he was often taken for younger than he was—and often took advantage of the mistake, so as to reap admiration for precocious brilliance. Unnecessarily, for indeed he was precociously brilliant. That was the foundation of his success.

He was enrolled in Robert Greenlees' art school in Ingram Street, Glasgow. The youngest brother John was apprenticed to a seedsman. Willie was already a clerk. Thus the pattern was established by which the brothers must work while Martin developed his talent. Nelly helped in the home, and Mrs Anderson took in a boarder.

William Anderson senior, his days as a shipper over, moved back from Guardbridge to Leuchars. In the 1871 census he is living alone in two rooms, occupation 'Railway station agent unemployed'.

A WRECK AT THE BAR.

Chapter 2—An Urban Adolescence 1868–77

'CLASSES WERE IN the mornings and evenings, the middle of the day being free. Thus I had a considerable amount of time upon my hands, and was often at my wits end to know how to fill it in.' In the course of filling his empty days, probably with empty pockets, Martin witnessed grimmer sights in Glasgow than he had ever encountered in rural Fife and sedate St Andrews.

Glasgow was booming and throbbing with industry. The flames of forges lit up the night sky; fumes from chemical works polluted the air; the constant gentle rain was black with soot and corrosive with sulphur. Great fortunes had once been made in cotton and sugar and tobacco—in fact, in the manufacture of every commodity brought from the New World to feed and clothe and inebriate Britain's industrial masses. Great fortunes were still being made, as railway engines built in Glasgow were delivered all over the world in Clyde-built ships. The city was a vortex sucking in manpower. From the Highlands and Islands they came, from Ayrshire and Perthshire, but chiefly from Ireland; to sicken and die of tuberculosis and typhoid and all the other diseases of malnutrition and overcrowding. Their poverty was indescribable.

The young art student from Fife could have used his abundant leisure to admire the architecture of new finance houses and shipping offices. More likely he dropped in at the nearby Law Courts for entertainment. There he found reporters listening to the never-ending catalogue of assault and theft, with the unfailing plea in mitigation that 'the panel was drunk at the time'. The reporters got grotesque stories for the foot of a page—'Laughter in Court'. Sometimes their reports treated the defendant with sympathy, more often they ridiculed him, or her. Drunken eruptions of violence, marital assaults, gruesome accidents and suicide were all matter for laughs. Martin was fascinated by the faces—the sullen, ugly, depraved, half-starved faces of dwellers in the world's worst slums, of people impoverished in every sense. His artist's eye caught gestures and attitudes, the poor man's cringe, the slattern's defiance, the policeman's lofty unconcern. He was storing up the stock of images that would electrify London in 1891. Moreover, while as an adolescent he may well have regarded the unfortunates on show as figures of fun, below that level, unconsciously, in one who claimed to have no interest in politics, a political attitude was forming.

Martin spent nearly ten of his formative years in and around Glasgow. On leaving art school he was apprenticed to Arthur, the calico printer, as a designer. Mother proudly preserved two of his dainty patterns for dress prints; they contrast strongly with the masculine vigour of his cartoons. After her death her son carefully annotated them for posterity.

Another souvenir of this period is a tiny notebook in which he entered in minute lettering, indistinguishable from type but executed with a paintbrush (as his note explains) a list of his pupils at Eastfield Sunday school, and the record of their erratic attendance. The boys were aged up to seventeen and he was only nineteen. They were rough lads, some of them miners; no doubt twice his size. As he taught them the lesson of the week his mind was invaded by irreverent pictures. After he told

TWO AT A SWEEP

them the story of Ruth gleaning in the field of Boaz he painted Ruth in rear view, bent double and amply upholstered. Let us hope some of his fun crept into the Bible stories, for his pupils had not much fun in their lives. Two of the boys were killed as they went down the pit at 5.30 one November morning. One was seventeen, the other an orphan of fourteen.

At the docks to meet his friend Weir, a marine engineer, Martin saw a woman trying to drown herself. Weir:

> succeeded in catching hold of the woman with a boathook. As soon as the woman had recovered her voice, she started calling out "I'll do it again, I'll do it again," so persistently that Weir, seeing his good work going for nothing, promptly pushed her down again, still retaining a grip of her back clothes. At her next appearance from the water, the woman repeated her catch phrase,

and just as promptly was pushed back into the none too savoury waters of the Clyde; and this went on until, at last, she had had enough of it. "That'll do," she said. "Right," said Weir, "and that'll tak the clockin aff ye." And with that he hauled her out.

This episode typifies the black humour that underlies many Cynicus sketches, where sympathy and understanding are suspended in the interests of a joke. Desperate flippancy to keep horror at bay? Or sheer insensitivity? Martin was always capable of both.

With money from home Mrs Anderson rented an eight-roomed house, Dechmont Villa, in Wellshot Drive, and moved her three sons and daughter into a pleasantly residential area of Cambuslang, out of sight and sound and smell of its coalmines and brickworks, dye works and quarries. It was an area of the professional and the prosperous, living in commodious mansions. Their neighbours were a clergyman and a rope and twine manufacturer. It would be a daily exercise for Martin to adjust between the bourgeois gentility of Wellshot Drive and that special social atmosphere of Glasgow, that presumption that we are all equal and all poor, and all in the soup together.

Youthful Enterprise

With amazing self-confidence he set about founding an art club to meet his own need for a place to meet other artists. 'The Glasgow Art Club was then in full swing, but it was much too grand a thing for a poor practitioner like myself.' He therefore inserted an advertisement in the papers: "Some artists wish to meet others to form an Art Club for mutual improvement." 'Once I had carried out my bold step I was overcome with trepidation, because it was only then that I seemed to remember my age—I was barely sixteen.' (He *looked* barely sixteen. He was in fact nineteen.)

Surprise and consternation grew together when the results of my rash insertion began to arrive. Answers flowed in. Deciding, however, that I was now fairly launched into the wide sea of my own making, I engaged a room in the Rainbow Hotel... and answered all my correspondents with a note of the time and meeting-place.

When the night arrived for the meeting I duly entered the Rainbow, and was shown into the Commercial Room. It was already nearly full, and there were others coming in. I never dreamt, however, that these were the "artists", and it was not until the boots put his head round the corner of the door and said, "The room is now ready for the artists," and everybody got up and began to make their way upstairs, that the full significance of my boldness descended on me. I think the sweat gathered on my brow then if ever it did. I was not only the youngest person in the room by many years, but, by reason of my rather puny stature, I was decidedly the smallest.

The idea of flight came into my mind, and I was hurriedly debating within myself as to whether I should not then and there resign my "membership", when I noticed a kindly gentleman whom I had observed sitting in the room was among the last going up the stair.

Running up after him, I caught him by the coat tails before he could pass into the room. To him I explained the situation. He listened politely and gravely with never the ghost of a smile on his face, and when he had heard me through said: "Leave the matter to me."

We then went into the meeting. He took the chair, sat me down on his right hand, and opened the meeting... It went through without a hitch... and by the end of the evening the St Mungo Art Club was in existence.

The club enabled him to meet other Glasgow artists, even such eminent painters as Guthrie and Lavery, and forge connections that would aid him through the first stages of his career.

This ability that the young man possessed to infuse others with a willingness to help him came to his rescue on many occasions. He would always be thus enterprising, for in spite of the modesty he laid claim to he had great self-confidence.

At Arthur's, he also discovered the enchantment of amateur dramatics. His employer liked to stage entertainments by the staff. With a change of clothes, Martin found he could assume at will a grander, wiser, or more amusing personality. Much of his life he would be playing a part, whether the *enfant terrible*, the *ingénu*, the Bohemian, the laird, or, eventually, the eccentric. He lived the parts until he no longer knew what was original and what assumed. To be unfailingly amusing would sometimes be a hard part to play, when his heart was leaden, but it bought popularity.

William Anderson senior now rejoined his family and in his late sixties found employment in Rutherglen paper-mill in the humble position of overseer. The appeals, refusals and negotiations that preceded his arrival are lost to us, but we may well doubt whether his sons and daughter, upwardly striving in the respectable atmosphere of Wellshot Drive, gave him much of a welcome. Poor William! He had spent his later life in the shadow of a superior woman, conscious that he fell short in whatever he did. For, however successful she was in drilling her children to do her credit, with her husband she failed.

Cynicus showed us the natty figure of the stationmaster and mentioned the 'shipper in a small way'. Thereafter, silence. The last picture of him we have comes, not from his son, but from his death certificate. In December 1875 he died of concussion. Not at once, or there would have been a report to the procurator fiscal. Where did it happen? On the street? At the foot of the stairs? We may imagine him carried up to bed unconscious, and his offspring tiptoeing about the house, dubiously raising an eyebrow to each other, interrogating Mother with a look. Then when it was over, when drawn blinds informed Wellshot

Drive of their grief, what feelings were there, expressed or unexpressed, of sorrow, relief, regret? Willie was present at the death, but Willie is silent. And Martin, who tells us so much about his friends and his triumphs, never mentions his father's death. Like the sundial, he marks only the sunny hours.

The following year, Annie having returned from teaching in Perth, Mrs and the Misses Anderson (Annie and Nelly), started a private school. They taught reading and writing, drawing, painting and piano. Thanks to their mother, all the Andersons were already proficient in such arts.

My eyes and thoughts to Heaven go,
I ne'er see common things below.

Martin, by 1877 president of the St Mungo Art Society, made his debut as a newspaper illustrator through, literally, a red herring. It was a characteristic exercise of wit, imagination, and self-advertisement: 'I took a page from *The Bailie* [a well-known Glasgow weekly], bought a red herring, and with all the accuracy of which I was capable reproduced the herring with my pencil and brush across the page. I then gave it the title of "Full-length Portrait of a Glasgow Magistrate".' (A bailie is a magistrate. A 'Glasgow bailie' was a salt herring.) Displayed in the workplace at Arthur's, it attracted the notice of a client who happened to have a bookshop in Queen Street. 'He was so amused he displayed the work in his window, where it occasioned some hilarity, and was actually bought.' It not only brought Martin Anderson to public notice and proved he could make people laugh; it also taught him how to attract publicity. He would repeatedly resort to the shop window ploy at critical times.

Best of all, Frederick Wickes, owner of three Glasgow papers, saw and liked the sketch. He commissioned the twenty-two-year-old to provide tiny illustrations for serial stories running in his *News of the Week*. That job lasted only eleven months, because the paper died. Martin did not mind much, for he disliked the drudgery of having to scratch his drawing on to the copper plates by hand. According to his own boast, he rebelled at it, and bumptiously told the proprietor he was 'not a mechanic'. (Perhaps that was after he lost the job.) At least he had broken into the world of newspaper illustration. Some years later, when a publisher of many titles decided to introduce illustrations to his dailies, he turned to Martin Anderson.

THE SCOTTISH LION

Chapter 3—To London 1878–79

BEFORE HE WOULD submit to the drudgery of newspaper illustration, however, Martin's wings had to be clipped. The years in Glasgow had gone well and he was making headway. But he did not want to become known as an illustrator, nor did he adequately value his comic talent. He yearned to be regarded as a landscape artist. He already practised two constrasting styles. One is improbably romantic, all spiky mountains and Gothic forests lit with an apocalyptic crimson glow. The other is classically simple, just sky and water in subtle, delicate colours. He was fascinated by light—sunrise, moonlight, sunset.

Soon he was exhibiting in Scottish galleries. Not only was his 'Ancient Mariner' shown and bought at Kirkcaldy, 'one of the biggest art collectors in Edinburgh' asked for a copy. The aspiring artist replied with great moral superiority that he 'did not believe it right to make and sell copies of what had already been bought in all good faith as an only example'. The connoisseur nevertheless made an appointment to meet him in St Andrews Square, Edinburgh. Along came the *ingénu*. '[I] saw a tall gentleman standing on the edge of the pavement with all the appearance of waiting on some one. I was still a young lad and rather timid of introducing myself, and I think I must have passed and repassed him before I plucked up the courage to ask him if he was Mr William Sanderson. "Yes," he said, evidently surprised to see so small and young a person.' In spite of the louche air of the rendezvous the connoisseur was a respectable Edinburgh town councillor and wealthy wine and spirits maker. He was so taken with the 'lad' he invited him to spend the summer holidays with him, his wife and numerous offspring in a Ferry Road mansion, took him round and introduced him to prominent artists. 'I returned from that holiday,' Martin recalled, 'with a large number of commissions.' These ambiguous encounters will continue.

In 1878 his painting, 'The Music Lesson', was accepted for the Royal Scottish Academy's annual exhibition. The title suggests the scene was the little school in Dechmont Villa. Mother was overjoyed. The acceptance vindicated her faith in him and in his siblings' sacrifice. He pardonably took it as proof that he was being recognised as a serious painter, and, in an access of that euphoria which carried him through so much, decided it was time to scale greater heights. His confidence in himself was to be sorely tried.

He was an ambitious young man of twenty-four with his mother's blessing but hardly a penny in his pocket when he decided to attempt his fortune in London. It was almost a northern tradition: Phil May made his way there a year later; J M Barrie would follow suit at the same age as Martin.

> The way I set about it was nothing if not in the traditional manner. I approached a friend in the railway service and told him of my intention. Could he help me? He did—to the extent of a ticket to Carlisle.
>
> From there I made my way to London on my own resources, arriving without any luggage and with only a few odd shillings in my pocket. It was enough, however, to procure me a night's lodgings in a house in Drury Lane where the tariff for a bed was a shilling a night.

Thus he first made the acquaintance of Drury Lane, the scene of his future triumph.

According to a contemporary description it made an insalubrious base: 'the foot passenger of a morning saw the dirt and refuse of the Lane strewn about with the fine picturesqueness begotten of having been thrown out of window. Then the cabbage-leaf and the old newspaper sweltered happily for weeks together, and an old boot would toss about for a twelvemonth, till the hobnails fell out and some hungry dog at last could eat it.'

Martin could not afford to be choosy. 'The next morning,' he said, 'having brought my paint box and sketch book with me, I set myself to earn my living.' In an 1894 interview in the *Sketch* he said he came to London 'to study art proper'. We can imagine him haunting the galleries, lost in wonder and envy before grand classical canvasses. His own work had to be rather different. 'Mostly I made sketches of scenes on the Thames, and hawked them round the art shops at a shilling a time. On occasion, I was driven, when I had no money in my pockets for a night's lodgings, to trying to sell them in the street by stopping a likely looking customer.'

There is a breathtaking innocence about this statement. One can visualise the reaction of the likely looking customer accosted on a London street by a handsome youth in artistic attire. Was Martin by now aware that his boyish charm and good looks could be turned to account? He wanted to be an artist. It seemed that older men would obligingly come to his assistance if he made a charming appeal for help.

One Saturday night, finding myself in Piccadilly with nothing in my pocket and a week's lodgings to pay, I stepped into a dealer's and offered him anything in my folio for the price of a shilling. He looked them over and found nothing to his taste, but while I was showing him my sketches there was a gentleman kept looking over his shoulder, and, when I went out, rather in despair at my failure, he was standing looking in at the window, so I took my courage in my hands, touched him on the arm and offered him, as I had offered the dealer, any in the collection for a shilling.

He took a cursory glance at my work, handed me his card, and told me to call on Monday morning at the address given. And that was the nearest I got to earning my supper that night.

The card bore a Richmond address and the name of an extremely well-to-do art patron.

However, I had to go back and pacify my landlady with promises, tell her of my supposed good fortune, and get to work for Monday.

On Sunday morning I took out and arranged the assortment of pictures I wanted to show him, and there was one in particular, a water-colour of a Thames sunset, that I thought the best of the collection and likely to earn me more than any other. Unfortunately it was still unfinished. I had run out of my favourite colour, crimson lake, and had had no money with which to buy a fresh supply. There seemed to be nothing to do but to leave it behind when I went to Richmond.

Of course he would run out of crimson lake, for his Thames was permanently on fire.

Then there occurred a rather peculiar incident.

I went for a walk down Euston Road, came to Gordon Square, and stood for a moment to admire the church. It was while I was standing there that the presence of a small white cube on the pavement immediately in front of the church caught my eye.

I bent down and picked it up.

It was a cube of paint that had evidently fallen from a child's paint box—and it was crimson lake!

I hurried home and set to work to finish my picture.

On Monday morning I was up before the city was stirring, and set off on the tramp to Richmond. It is a long walk, as anyone who knows his London will vouch for, but it was a particularly long one for a man who had no food in his stomach. When I came to the address on the card I found it to be one of the very fine houses that occupy the river bank there, laid out amid beautifully-kept gardens and with green-carpet lawns running down to the water.

I was received by a flunkey and shown into a room, where my patron sat. We talked for some minutes and were in the midst of our conversation when a chef or head-cook walked in with a silver tray and a silver bowl, in which there steamed some soup, probably the most fragrant, sweetest-promising soup that ever assailed the human nostrils.

My mouth watered. I prepared myself to deal with it.

The chef handed it to his master. The master tasted it.

"Yes," he said, "that will do very well for tonight." And the chef walked out with the soup.

However, I sold my crimson lake sunset and some other sketches, and left with five pounds in my pocket, richer than I had been for months.

Straightway, I went and had something to eat. Then I bought a postal order, retired to the seclusion of the Kew Churchyard, and there sat down on a tombstone to pretend to my mother through the medium of the postal order and the letter I wrote that I was veritably making my fortune in London.

When I had finished writing I looked at the stone on which I sat and found that it was the tomb of Gainsborough.

So many coincidences must have confirmed him in the belief that he was destined to be a serious artist.

He stuck at it. 'I was lucky enough eventually to please the management of a big art firm near King's Cross, and was thereafter kept in fairly steady employment, though my earnings were never more

BROTHERS OF THE BRUSH.

than sufficient to meet my daily needs.' By one of those indirect hints we find in the memoirs we gain some idea of what kept him in steady employment. 'There was a group of artists then... who had a unique job. They were all of them impecunious at that time, although since then some of their names have become extremely well known.' And some of them eventually frequented his famous studio in Drury Lane.

> As artists in need of any money they could make they were extremely useful to two publishers of the time who carried on a sideline in "antiques". The process was this. They hired these artists to copy Old Masters, then subjected the copies to a faking system that included cracks, dullness, dust and whatever was required to make them look like the real thing.
>
> Agents were employed in various parts of the more remote country, and to these the Old Masters were despatched. Their business was to plant the pictures in some cottage or farm where the owner was willing to subscribe to the fraud, and then, when sufficient time had elapsed to allow the dust and cobwebs to settle, the Old Masters were duly "discovered".

Characteristically, Cynicus made light of the hardship and disappointment that he suffered in that year, preferring to dwell on a stroke of luck that netted him five pounds in Richmond. But it was a bitter experience being an impecunious artist, and not easily forgotten.

Daumier?

Cynicus recorded one other episode from this unsuccessful period in London:

> I was then occupying a garret near King's Cross for which I paid two shillings and sixpence a week. And it was there that I received a visit from my three wealthy cousins, the Campbells of the Perth dyeworks, on their way to Paris to the Exhibition.
>
> They left fully convinced that I was living in affluent circumstances, for my landlady had had the good sense to show them in to her best sitting-room and not up to my half-crown attic.

Grateful to be spared the ignominy of having his poverty revealed, Martin soon scored a small triumph over the well-to-do cousins. He went to Paris too. 'Their visit had one effect on me. It determined me that I should also see the Exhibition, though I had only fifteen shillings to my name—I think this must be one of the most economical pieces of foreign travel ever undertaken.'

He stayed five days, sleeping rough, washing in a fountain, and getting breakfast 'from the men who used to perambulate the streets with a canister of soup on their backs'. Sleeping rough did not mean neglecting his appearance; he carried a supply of clean collars inside his hat. Unfortunately he forgot this when he entered the Church of the Madeleine, devoutly swept off his hat, and saw his spruce future cascade to the floor and roll about under the feet of the worshippers. Devotion to good grooming overpowered the religious kind. To the amusement of the congregation he scrabbled about under their feet until he recovered the lot. On his return to London he plumed himself on finding that 'for my fifteen shillings I had seen more of Paris than my three cousins put together'.

The legacy of this escapade was not a love of foreign travel. It was the experience of sleeping under a park bush and waking to birdsong, the smell of grass and flowers and the plashing of a fountain, that gave him a lasting vision of gypsy freedom he would long to recapture.

He did not describe his visit to the Exhibition. We surmise he visited another exhibition, one that determined his future career. His later work rather suggests that he saw the great retrospective exhibition of Daumier cartoons. As an immature young man and a foreigner, he probably passed by without understanding the serious political work. One hooded mourning figure did sink into his unconscious to reappear years later as 'Futurity' in the first 'Satires of Cynicus'. What took his fancy at that age would be the 'Emotions Parisiennes', the incongruity between the ideal and the actual, the slapstick accidents of snow or flower pots or water falling on the heads of passersby, of mayhem lurking round the next corner. Unable to make much of the lengthy captions in French he appreciated the energy of movement in the drawing. We suspect from that time on it primed his invention.

In the end Martin abandoned the premature attempt to force his talent on London, and headed for home. London

An Eavesdropper.

had beaten him for the present, but secretly he swore to return and succeed. It took twelve years to amass the weapons wherewith to conquer the metropolis—not the few months the metropolis imagined. Even while he appeared to be moving in another direction the resolve was still there.

Chapter 4—By Our Staff Artist 1880–85

ALTHOUGH CYNICUS PRESENTS himself as the traditional Bohemian starving in a garret the fact that he returned to Cambuslang via Dundee suggests a streak of sober bourgeois commonsense. He may have gone to apply for a job.

At all events, he was soon invited by John Leng & Co, the Dundee newspaper publisher, to join the *Dundee Advertiser* as its staff artist, the first to be employed by any daily paper in Britain. Up till then, the daily press was unillustrated.

John Leng was a left-wing Liberal. His papers—the *Dundee Advertiser,* the *Evening Telegraph,* the *People's Journal,* and the *People's Friend*—aimed to educate the working class. Studying their columns, Martin absorbed ideas about free education and universal suffrage, the need to take the land from private landlords and the iniquity of imperialism.

To take up the new appointment meant returning to the East of Scotland. Possibly Willie was already in Dundee when Martin visited it; more likely he obediently gave up his job in the West to help his younger brother. Willie became a commercial traveller in the provision trade. At first he and Martin stayed with their maiden aunt and two sisters in the little town of Tayport, travelling daily to Dundee by the Tay ferries. Their mother and the other three children remained for a little in Cambuslang, keeping the school going and taking in lodgers, till the brothers were able to rent half of a villa close to Dundee, in Hill Street, Broughty Ferry. Then the Cambuslang party rejoined them. Marion and Lizzie remained with their aunt in Tayport, just across the water.

Broughty Ferry, their new home, was a new Cambuslang. Nobody stayed in Dundee if he could help it. The prosperous citizens built their mansions in Broughty and took little pride in the city that provided their wealth. Glasgow had prestigious public buildings; Dundee had jute mills. Women and children supplied cheap labour, while their men lounged on street corners, unemployed and demoralised. As the poor poured into the city there was the same overcrowding, the same degraded population of country folk and Irish immigrants as in Glasgow, the same ravages of disease. In a splendid natural situation, between heather hills and a noble estuary, the city consisted largely of tenements with their back courts filled in with more tenements until the inhabitants gasped for air. Willie and Martin came up by train from their salubrious suburb and plunged into the maze of alleys that led them to their workplaces in adjacent streets.

Martin's first sketches appeared in the middle of 1880. The *Dundee Advertiser* required largely topographical and architectural subjects. Over the following years he sketched a fair number of churches, castles, new buildings, statues and conflagrations. As staff artist he travelled about the locality on assignments.

One such took him to Meigle to draw newly discovered Pictish stones. The local joiner who had reported them surprisingly turned out to have taught himself Greek and Hebrew. He asked the young reporter to take an interest in his nephew, William Craigie. In due course Craigie became a regular visitor to the Andersons' house and a valued friend. Unlike his uncle, the nephew was able to make full use of his talent. He wound up as Sir William Craigie, professor at Oxford and Chicago. Many of his letters express his admiration for Cynicus's work, the young man looking up to the elder.

Another assignment took him to Balmoral after the death of Queen Victoria's favourite, John Brown, since a rumour was circulating that the Queen in her grief had erected an 'unusually conspicuous stone' over his grave in Crathie Churchyard. The staff artist had just settled down in the churchyard with his sketchbook when a carriage drove up to the gates and the Queen descended.

She entered the yard unattended. I had just the necessary time to hide myself behind a tombstone before she appeared. She approached the tomb slowly, drew up a wire garden chair that was placed there for her and sat down facing the stone. Leaning her head on her hand she sat gazing at the grave with an expression of resigned sadness.

For half an hour she sat thus, while I, but two or three yards away, trembled lest she should discover me. For the making of a sketch, however, the opportunity was too good to lose, and before she left I had not only the tomb of John Brown, but his chief mourner...

The Queen was then having erected in front of her drawing-room window a statue of her trusty Brown, but when she died and King Edward ascended the throne it was quickly removed.

Needless to say, the *Dundee Advertiser* published a sketch of the Brown family gravestones and not an unofficial portrait of Queen Victoria.

What had brought Martin to Leng's attention in the first place were his tiny illustrations in Glasgow's *News of the Week*. For the serial stories in Leng's *Evening Telegraph* he was allowed about three thumbnail sketches per instalment. The space was cramped, the range of subjects limited, yet already they exhibited some of those features which were to characterise his picture postcards of the early 1900s; such as the top-hatted man pursued by a bull, and the housewife in mutch and shawl. The young artist enjoyed embarrassing situations: a lady lost her wig in company; a dignified gent took a tumble; a drunk clung to a lamp post. The figures were caught in mid-action, in ridiculous attitudes, their surprise and fury captured in a few lines.

One story, the *Blunders of a Bashful Man,* was also published as a sixpenny booklet, with Martin given credit for the illustrations. Other booklets followed. *Humorous Readings Maistly Scotch* ran to seventeen editions in a few years. The Cynicus style of energetic movement was developing fast. It was about to develop its full potential.

Quiz

When Martin left Glasgow in 1880, friends were talking of launching a comic weekly. When the magazine *Quiz* came out in the spring of 1881, it claimed to employ 'the cleverest young artists we could find for a weekly supply of sketches illustrative of local scenes or social subjects' and writers 'who have already won their spurs on the literary battlefield'. Martin was in on it from the start. This was the single most important event in his life. When his first two books, the *Satires of Cynicus* and *Humours of Cynicus,* burst upon London within a space of six months, critics were amazed at the speed of his invention and execution. *Quiz* supplies the explanation.

Punch began as an imitation of the Parisian *Charivari,* and *Quiz* began as an imitation of *Punch.* So we deduce from the cover, where a world of tiny figures disports itself, as on the original cover of *Punch.* The cover was Martin's work.

For a self-proclaimed Liberal paper it soon became remarkably anti-everything: anti-Irish, anti-crofter, anti-Salvation Army, anti-Gladstone, anti-Randolph Churchill, anti-suffragette. It presented a parochial self-satisfied middle-class image. The readers of *Quiz* were presumed to own fine houses in the new suburbs and send wife and children away for the summer to resorts on the Firth of Clyde, far from the city epidemics. The working class on their July holiday, 'Fair Setturday', went 'doon the watter' too, on steamers with German bands and Highland pipers and an ever-open bar, but they were presumed not to be readers, and could therefore safely be held up to ridicule.

As *enfants terribles* the youthful staff specialised in heartless witticisms about the misfortunes of the urban poor, such as suggesting that washing-tubs had been invented by Providence to drown their surplus children. But on one occasion a reporter sent to discover the 'sinful secrets' of Glasgow's slums returned temporarily chastened to write:

> For unmitigated squalor, absolute lack of furniture, and sign after sign of reckless degradation, and hopeless misery, and sheer brutality, they surpass anything you can imagine without having seen. Saddest of all it was to see

the children who played merrily about these haunts of liquor-drenched vice. "Twym" has drawn a little lass who opened a door to us. Her regular features, deep blue eyes and wealth of silky hair, should have been a mother's pride. But the mother was lying drunk on a heap of rags in a corner—and the rags were all the furniture of the room.

'Twym' was A S Boyd. While his regular contribution was a page of topical illustrations from the Glasgow theatres, largely appreciative of girls' legs, and a plentiful supply of humorous sketches, he was privately of a more serious cast of mind. After Henry George's tour of Scotland preaching land nationalisation, Twym published a bitter cartoon with as title George's watchword, 'Land for the People'. It showed a graveyard. (Cynicus used this idea himself much later to great effect, when 'Land for the People' became his own war cry.)

Confined to illustrating other men's ideas—in the *Dundee Advertiser*, with dry, faithful representations of public buildings, and in the other Leng papers, with minute sketches—Martin turned to this work with relief. A dammed-up stream of creativity burst forth. For seven years from the magazine's inception he contributed weekly at least one and sometimes as many as three cartoons.

Dramatis Personae

His weekly offerings, signed with a monogram of MA, rang the changes on a number of themes. He invented a population of doleful thin men in battered top hats and tattered gloves, of skinny spinsters with marital

AN UNFORTUNATE ATTACHMENT.

THE TRANSIT OF VENUS.

hopes or artistic pretensions, natty young men, nice tubby old couples, decrepit ancients with aspirations to courtship, cannibals and 'Black Sambos', working-class viragos in carpet slippers and great frilled caps, charging bulls and goats, vocal cats, howling babies and their demented fathers, naughty boys and haughty policemen.

A favourite theme is the mishap that deflates a solemn occasion. As the mourner leaves, dabbing a handkerchief to his eyes, his coat tail catches in the door, giving 'A Parting Tear'. Sombrely clad missionaries take to their heels when their black brothers turn out to be cannibals intent on 'Dispatching Foreign Mails'. MA enjoys the discomfiture of the prim and stuffy when some accident causes them to erupt into unbecoming antics. A raging bull charges into a peaceful picnic party and scatters the participants. The landscape, easel, palette and artist tossed in the air by a berserk cow give us 'Away ye Gay Landscapes!' We laugh at the comic twist supplied by a pun or misapplied literary quotation. When a child drops from an apple-tree on to spiked railings to illustrate 'Something to Fall Back Upon' we recognise the black humour of the *enfants terribles*. Apart from the accidents and disappointments that beset the ordinary man, MA ridicules the hypocrite, the belligerent slum dweller, and the aged who trespass on the prerogatives of youth. MA is indulgent to the lone swaying drunk with his affection for lamp posts, and hard on the violent parent. He occasionally presents a murderous Irish patriot and the native Glasgow tough. Urchins pursue their mischief throughout, tripping up the respectable passerby, stealing apples and jam, being nabbed by the copper, or feeling the weight of a maternal hand.

For the male, life begins with squalling, proceeds through a childhood of being cuffed and whacked for misdemeanours, to the bliss of courtship (too often thwarted), into the warfare of matrimony and the purgatory of parenthood, till the decrepit ancient tries to recapture his youth by wooing a pretty girl. For the female, matrimony brings a drunken husband, domestic quarrels and violence. Again and again he portrays the vengeful wife lying in wait for the drunk's return. The degrading effect of alcohol is a constant topic. The Saturday soak becomes the Sunday hypocrite. 'The Transit of Venus' shows a woman in a drunken stupor being trundled away by the police on their handcart. He reworked the idea into the roaring drunken matron of a later cartoon of the same name.

Memories of the Law Courts give him the virago shaking her fist at the JP ('Swearing before a Magistrate') and the woman with black eye and bandaged head who illustrates a purple patch from Thomas Moore—

If tenderness touched her, the dark of her eye
At once took a darker, a heavenlier dye.

(The poet was asking for it.) A tough in a similar condition has his eye 'Closed for Repairs'.

Being instinctively on the side of the underdog, Martin allows illtreated animals their revenge. Dogs bite, bulls and goats attack, insects sting, cats yowl all night. Young Martin also allows the elderly their love and courtship, provided they keep within their own age group. The treatment is whimsical, with never a trace of impropriety. At this stage we do not know whether that is *Quiz* policy or the artist's own.

He seems to have been counselled (by Mother?) to stick to safe targets. He never expresses an overt political viewpoint; perhaps so far he had none. He does tilt at organised religion, whether the Church of Scotland continually begging for money or clerics of different sects who cut each other on the street. Roman Catholics were considered fair game; so we have lazy, gluttonous monks and—the closest he came to anything indecorous—'Amor Vincit Omnes' (Love Conquers All). The *Quiz* version has a glamorous nun making eyes at a monk over the top of her Bible; in a later version they are kissing.

What strikes one about this early work is that the picture tells the story. So many cartoonists, even now, depend on the caption—and in Victorian times it was a lengthy caption—to deliver the joke, while the cartoon itself is often otiose. Covering up the caption reveals that the picture tells nothing. Martin Anderson's drawings are amusing in their own right. The caption only adds another comic element, by the

The Wolf & the Lamb

incongruity between a poetic quotation and the ludicrous scene it is applied to. The Victorians were very fond of puns; *Quiz* is full of them.

From 1881 onwards he provided a regular cartoon entitled 'British Classics Illustrated'. 'Voices of the night.—Longfellow': a man in a nightshirt holds two screaming babes while cats shriek outside. The touch of a vanished hand.—Tennyson': a weeping urchin feels his behind. The technique is infectious. Once one is alerted, common sayings take on grotesque interpretations. Perverting the original meaning becomes a game.

In paying tribute to his mother, Anderson mentioned her predilection for quotations. 'In those days there were no dictionaries of quotations, and we have volumes of well-known quotations from authors and poets with date, line and verse noted.' He inherited those books, and to judge from his use of the present tense ('we *have* volumes') treasured them into his late seventies. They were undoubtedly well-thumbed, for it remained one of Cynicus's favourite devices, from *Quiz* to the Cynicus Publishing Company Ltd, to create pictorial puns with popular quotations, whether from Byron or Mrs Hemans, Shakespeare or music-hall songs.

Throughout the years when the family lived together in Broughty Ferry they must have helped Martin a great deal with the weekly ideas. What occurred to one of them in the course of the day would be presented to him when he came home in the evening. One can picture them all sitting round the lamplit table after tea, enjoying the joke, suggesting improvements, bowing to Mother's verdict. Martin's joyous self-confidence grew in the atmosphere of approval.

Thanks to *Quiz* and Leng's publications, Martin had unwittingly found his forte. He discovered he was a born cartoonist. To quote him against himself, 'A blind man could scarcely have avoided observing the fact that there was one direction in which I had a bent'.

Ladies of the Court.   Swearing before a Magistrate.

Chapter 5—Getting Into His Stride 1886–90

THE SUCCESS OF the little humorous booklets put out by J Leng & Co decided Martin to produce one himself. *Miss Magdalen Green's Grand Tour* was all his own work—he conceived the ideas, wrote a text, and drew the illustrations. Printed on his employer's presses, it appeared in the middle of 1886. The 'Grand Tour' is an amusing title in itself, for the tour took at most a day, while Magdalen Green is a Dundee park.

The *Dundee Advertiser,* very likely in the person of Martin, for his style is unmistakable, gave it a glowing review: 'It is short but awfully sweet... Miss Green, after an introductory poem well fitted to drive McGonagall mad with envy, meanders gently round all the principal sights, giving curious historical, anecdotical, and enigmatical information.' 'She' poked gentle fun at local institutions, pastimes and people. There were jibes at the apathy of Tayport when a local landowner simply appropriated common land, local details no doubt gleaned from his Tayport aunt and sisters. *Miss Magdalen Green's Grand Tour* ran to at least three editions. His mother did not live to see his first production. She had died in March 1886, but no doubt saw it in embryo.

By Christmas he had produced—and favourably reviewed—a sequel, *Miss Magdalen Green's Christmas*: 'Jokes, stories, puns, conundrums, all beautifully and appropriately illustrated by the clever pencil of the spinster, abound. It is an astonishing pennyworth.'

Although these little booklets were themselves ephemeral, illustrations from them became highly popular over twenty years later when reworked as picture postcards.

After Mrs Anderson's death Willie, Martin, Annie and Nelly all left Broughty Ferry together and moved back across the Tay. Though the hand of authority was removed, their mother had a lasting influence on them. She kept them together. She gave Martin's career its direction. She made them subordinate their own careers to his. One wonders how much of Martin's career was in the interests of piously pleasing Mother.

In his drawings Martin depicted relations between the sexes, but had none himself. His brothers and sisters were no different. It was as if their childhood experiences had turned them against matrimony. They determined to steer clear of it, unlike the poor fools lampooned in Martin's sketches. Or again, they may have developed an exaggerated sense of family identity, of 'specialness' that excluded outsiders. Mrs Anderson was a woman of strong character. She may have so stunted her children's emotional growth that they could never break out of the closed family circle and form adult relationships, which would be seen as treachery to the group. Not one of the seven did marry, except Nelly as she approached fifty. In a mutual support system they remained bound to each other.

In Tayport four of them took a seven-roomed cottage in Broad Street, called Grovebank, and all moved in. The sisters Marion and Lizzie lived nearby in the grandparents' old house with their aunt, Ann Martin. She made her half of the family estate available to repay bonds. As the sole survivor of the older generation she took the position of parent to her sister's children. Only John, the youngest, briefly broke away from the group and returned to Glasgow.

'Cynicus' is Born

The stream of cartoons kept coming. From 1884 Martin no longer signed his *Quiz* sketches with the MA monogram, but instead with the pseudonym 'Bob'.

In November 1887 he adopted a second pseudonym. 'Bob' still provided the comic element; spinsters were still old, ugly and hopeful; drink still brought the lower orders to blows. But in his new independence of maternal control he spread his wings. He drew the first 'Satires of Cynicus'. Significantly, the first instalment of 'Satires' presented a sketch without words—man and wife in the form of a candle and a snuffer—a comment on his parents' relationship that he would not previously have dared to express. This became one of Martin's own favourites, perhaps because he had early resolved not to let marriage snuff out his individuality. 'Cynicus' introduced new themes. He moved away from safe and trivial targets into the dangerous and powerful realm of politics.

MAN AND WIFE.

He got into his stride with two sketches that, once reworked, became classics—'Capital and Labour' and 'A Lawsuit'. Both are strong, symmetrical compositions. The first shows the burly plutocrat Capital supported on the straining shoulders of his workers. The second shows the lawyer between wrangling litigants, with his hands in both their pockets. 'The Threshold of Our Faith' is a church doorway with the collection plate barring entry. 'Bob' was given credit for 'Faith Hope Charity'—the poor man mounts the steps to a house door in faith and hope, only to be booted back down by charity. 'The Modern Prometheus' is the poet weighed down by debt and attacked by harpy creditors. In February 1888 came the two purses, the full purse swelling with confidence, the empty one cringing.

Martin Anderson was just developing the Cynicus attributes. He had not yet evolved the distinctive signature. Some symbols would be dropped, such as Diogenes writing in a tub, while others would be retained for the rest of his days. The punning emblem of 'Truth the lyre' was eventually carved in sandstone over the entrance to Castle Cynicus.

The 'Satires of Cynicus' appeared in *Quiz* up to March 1888. Then followed cartoons entitled 'Romance and Reality by Cynicus'. These depicted the gulf between aspiration and actuality. 'This is the brave soldier who went to fight for Fame and Glory, And this is what he brought home'—a wooden leg. After May cartoons were signed simply C or Bob, the last appearing in August. Twym had already left *Quiz* to join the competition, the *Bailie*. The best days of *Quiz* were over.

A Bold Leap

Cynicus, as we may now call him, was in a fairly comfortable position on a good salary. If his employment was wearisome he had found better outlets for his talent. Just as, in Glasgow, the St Mungo Art Club had supplemented the Glasgow Art Society, so in Dundee the Art Club gathered those who did not feel at home in the Art Union. In 1884 Martin was secretary, in 1886 treasurer, in 1888 president. It gave him an opportunity for the romantic painting he loved and encouragement from new friends. Apart from himself its best-known member was his assistant and successor at Leng's, John Duncan, the painter of Celtic mythology.

Of this period a friend later wrote: 'In Dundee streets no figure was more conspicuous. Though he was not big in stature, the brisk beady-eyed artist compelled notice. He was a live wire, flying along with his Highland cloak blowing about him. He radiated fun. In a somewhat squeaky voice he distributed the best of humour. He could tell stories in an exquisitely droll way. In the best sense of the term he was a "comic".'

After the success of his little books about 'Miss Magdalen Green' Cynicus felt he was cut out for greater things. It was time to produce another book of his own. Since he had never forgotten his resolve to get even with London he would have it published there. In *Quiz* he had a

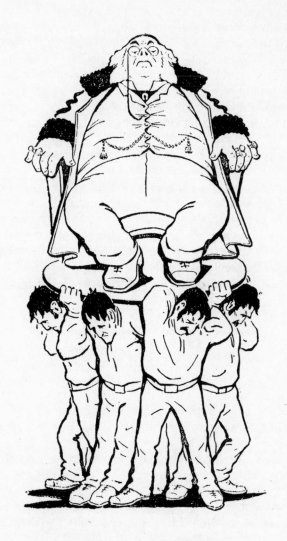

CAPITAL & LABOUR.

wealth of material to choose from. Importantly, he had contributed to *Quiz* as a free-lance artist, so when he chose to rework or simply re-use his ideas, he was free to do so. The pictures would have to be redrawn, of course, because, though the ideas were his, the actual printing blocks belonged to *Quiz*. All the time that he was pouring out new material for *Quiz* he must have been revising and refining his earlier work.

The new attack on London was well thought out. Cynicus decided on quarto pages, as most convenient for both full-page cartoons and a layout of two to four smaller sketches to a page. The cartoon collection would consist of six monthly parts, each part to contain two full-page cartoons ready for mounting. Even if these were all removed—and few purchasers would want to frame them all—forty-eight pages of drawings would remain to bind as a book.

He selected from his existing sketches, redrew them to the new size, cutting out everything superfluous, until only the outline was left. Occasionally he added clarifying detail, strengthened the line, improved the literary allusion and sharpened the effect.

Since Cynicus fancied himself as a versifier, he included rhyming couplets and quatrains and a few longer poems. Apart from the pithy couplets there is an abundance of archaic *'t will*s and *'t would*s.

He mulled over subjects for eye-catching new cartoons. Something contentious ought to attract notice; that he had learned. Since he was printing this collection privately, he could please himself. He chose to use almost all the controversial subjects from the *Quiz* 'Satires of Cynicus' and add more in similar vein. His inspiration caught the new spirit of the age. Gossip writers fished in a cesspool of slander; a fat middleman intercepted the food of his skinny victims; the rich boy mounted the poor boy's back to pick an apple, then sat out of reach to eat it; human society, led by Establishment figures, raced after the devil's coin; the old and gouty, led by a figure in royal robes, pursued a scantily clad chorus girl.

Blocks were made from his sketches and printed in Ludgate Hill, London. Publication was entrusted to D R Duncan at the *Dundee Advertiser's* Fleet Street office.

Cynicus is not one to share the glory; he claims he struck on the felicitous notion of colouring in the prints. When in due course the prints arrived at Tayport, the sisters set to work to tint them by hand. They little knew what they were taking on. They started with eight insipid watercolour shades, then built up the relief with deeper tones. Delightedly they filled in the printed outlines.

The family debated how much to charge. Should the ordinary edition be offered in twelve fortnightly instalments at threepence each or in six monthly instalments at sixpence? What about an edition de luxe in

PRINCIPLE AND INTEREST.

monthly parts at one-and-a-penny each, individually retouched? All of these, for early subscribers.

The first subsciptions were solicited from Fife and Dundee friends. As publication date approached the family was in a state of high excitement. Each day they eagerly awaited word from London.

Time went past and nothing happened. No subscriptions.

No rave reviews. No reviews at all. Silence.

What had gone wrong? What could they have overlooked?

Between rage and disbelief Cynicus saw his second attempt to conquer London ignored. He was heavily out of pocket. Although there had been advertisements in his 'Miss Magdalen Green' booklets, this time the artist in his hubris had declared on the cover of the first instalments: 'This is a unique effort to start a periodical without the aid of empiric advertisements.' He had paid for paper and printing and paint. Annie and Nelly were to have a share of the profits. Even bad reviews would have signalled interest. But to be totally ignored!

He went to London to find out for himself. 'I called upon my publishers, and found that with the exception of what I had been able to sell privately, practically nothing had been done with the "Satires".'

Seemingly D R Duncan regarded the production of a book at the author's expense as vanity publishing, so he had nothing to do with marketing. That was the author's business.

In 1890 Martin is recorded as a council member of the Dundee Art Club, but there is reason to think that he had already taken the gamble of giving up his secure job with Leng, and decamped to London. 'It was no easy break, for my salary then was £250 a year, as much if not more than was being paid anywhere in the provinces for newspaper illustration. It had become obvious to me, however, that if I was to make any proper headway in the world, I must recommence my attack on London.' He had drawn enough ancient piles in the East of Scotland; now he would get his own ideas into the public eye.

Martin Anderson was 35 years old. Despite a previous taste of poverty in London, his ambition was matched by faith in his abilities. This time he had friends to stay with. He sent for Nellie and racked his brains for a plan of action.

THE AUTHOR AND THE PUBLISHER.

Chapter 6—The Great Adventure 1890–91

HOW COULD HE get his pictures noticed? He had no influential friends or contacts. He had no paid employment now and little money to see him through. He would have to rely on his own ingenuity and rise to fame on a shoestring.

It is not clear how long he spent deliberating the means to engineer publicity (he generally suggested it was only a few weeks), but the story of how he did it was often retold. One morning in early spring 1891 the little man was making his way up a seedy sidestreet off the Strand, perhaps recalling the splash he had made in Glasgow when his 'Full-length Portrait of a Glasgow Magistrate' was exhibited in a shop window. Before he had gone far up Drury Lane his eye lit on a 'To Let' sign above a small shop.

The premises had obviously once been a fried fish shop, but as he looked at it he disregarded its squalid surroundings and perceived a large display window in a busy thoroughfare, on the doorstep of innumerable theatres, not far from the Law Courts and Fleet Street, on a route running directly to the British Museum. Although it was a slum, Drury Lane was not far from the haunts of the professional and well-to-do. Moreover, it was all he could afford.

For London it was in fact cheap. The rent for the shop was ten shillings a week and a further six and sixpence could provide economical living accommodation in small upstairs rooms. The deal was struck. The artist and his sister straightaway took up residence at 59 Drury Lane. It was a thrill to be at the hub of Empire, the centre of British culture, but there was no time to waste on self-congratulation. The premises had to be cleaned up and all traces of fried fish removed before they could serve as an artist's studio.

'I ... spent Saturday and Sunday preparing the shop-front and the window. [No word of Nelly scrubbing.] First of all, however, I called on the publisher and removed all the printed copies of the "Satires". It was these that I placed in my curtained window preparatory to ringing up on the Monday morning.' As an act of faith he boldly painted 'Cynicus Publishing Company' over the door. The story goes that he had got no further than 'Cynicus Pub' when Scots friends chanced along. Shortly after, according to him, it was rumoured in Dundee that he had opened a public house.

Cynicus recalled: 'Promptly at nine o'clock on the Monday morning I rang up the curtain. An hour later a policeman came in and said I would have to take my pictures out of the window. They had caused a crowd to collect that was holding up the street traffic. I argued it with him, however, that it was his job to keep the street clear, not mine, and eventually he laughed, became good friends, and allowed the display to go on.' Cynicus had considerable personal charm.

What is nowhere mentioned in this tale is the part played by the elder brother William. Yet William resigned his job in Dundee and joined Martin and Nelly to give them the benefit of his business sense. If Martin found the shop, it was probably William who arranged the lease. As ever, it was a family affair. The reason for blotting out William will appear later.

An Instant Celebrity

Very soon they had to send off for more coloured sheets from Annie in Tayport, for the *Satires of Cynicus* had attracted instant attention. As an erstwhile friend remarked, 'Dwellers in the Lane had not much money to spend on pictures, nor anything else for that matter, so at first he had to depend upon casual passers-by. But it was not long before there were collectors of his telling cartoons... Lawyers from the Courts near by were his best buyers.' Word spread quickly.

In Tayport Annie was unable to cope. What was required was a workforce organised to colour the prints for them, but they would have

A LAW SUIT.

44

to find workers, then teach and supervise them. Cynicus claimed he hit on the solution. Annie had art training. She had become a teacher when the family split up, so she could certainly handle children. Why should she not train a few of those children who had left school without finding employment? The local jute factory was the only female employment in Tayport. It took a robust physique to run to and fro all day with cops of thread for the weavers, to creep about under the looms sweeping up the dust, with the prospect of eventually standing at a loom for twelve hours a day. In Tayport were youngsters who had been rejected as unsuitable by the factory, or whose parents were loath to send them there. This was the germ of the venture which at its peak constituted an important Tayport industry.

At the London end the first numbers were selling as fast as they arrived from Scotland.

It is proof of the extraordinary originality and power of his cartoons that first-class publications at once sought to employ him. One of the first callers was Charles Morley, the editor of *Pall Mall Budget*. In the dirty slum that was Drury Lane he found a brightly painted little shop. Invited to sit in the 'studio' he was served with tea by a diminutive young woman. The satirist turned out to be an elegant little person apparently just out of his teens. Spick and span, handsome and witty, he sparkled, beguiled and charmed. Morley found himself offering a commission to supply the weekly *Pall Mall Budget* with humorous cartoons. Cynicus lent some of the printing blocks and as a result had an art notice of two full pages. Morley quoted the *Satires'* frontispiece: '"Cynicus" asks no favour, is no partisan; independent and unbiassed, he looks with impartial eye on the follies and corruptions of his time. Unknown and unaided, but with firm purpose, he launches his satires on a world of dissimulation and deceit.' Morley added: 'With this brief introduction, which explains the spirit of Mr. Anderson's work, we give a few of the sketches which appear in the book, the price of which, by the way, is a guinea.' The price had doubled already.

The week after he had been 'discovered', Cynicus began providing cartoons for the *Pall Mall Budget*. They appeared sporadically from March to October 1891 and occasionally in the following year, and one can follow Cynicus's own sightseeing around London: the University Boat Race, Easter holiday scenes at Hampstead Heath, at the Surrey Theatre, the National Gallery, Bow Street, at St Paul's. Once or twice he drew on his handy supply of *Quiz* sketches.

Hot on the heels of Morley came Sidney Low, the editor of *St James's Gazette*. He offered a handsome £600 per annum for Cynicus to become his Lobby artist, but Cynicus had just spent years as a staff artist in Dundee. He would gladly take on commissions, but drew the line at becoming an employee again.

Many years later, he gave two reasons for rejecting the generous offer: 'I turned it down—firstly, because I was not—and never have been—interested in politics; secondly, and more particularly, because the one thing I have always avoided is portraiture. And this is where I disagree with the modern cartoonist, who cannot draw a cartoon but he must have it filled with recognisable portraits. The result cannot be anything else but ephemeral. Other offers followed of illustrative work and so on, but I had found what suited me admirably, and I was satisfied.'

With scarcely an exception Cynicus stuck to portraying types, not individual personalities, so that his work would be permanent when that of others was passé. A glance through magazines of the Nineties bears him out. Caricatures of dead politicians leave us cold. Eternal types touch our imagination. It seems odd that Cynicus, who even called one of his books *Cartoons Social and Political,* should deny any interest in politics, but he had a reason.

The *St James's Gazette* gave him an ecstatic review:

> That "Cynicus" can wield the tomahawk, the bludgeon, the scalping knife, or the cutting whip with wonderful dexterity, is as plain as a pikestaff directly one opens his handsome volume …Stronger work, in outline, has not often been done; but, indeed, for mastery of line and felicity of suggestion, "Cynicus" stands by himself in contemporary English caricature. His balanced, but spontaneous union of vigour with absolute simplicity, his mordant satire, his strong individuality, and his gift of that ideality without which there is no art, mark him out as a caricaturist of very high rank.

This review brought a stream of customers to Drury Lane.

The novelist Israel Zangwill was another early caller at the studio. At the beginning of 1891 he had launched another rival to *Punch,* called *Ariel or the London Puck.* When Cynicus became an instant celebrity, Zangwill realised that the newcomer could give his publication a boost. From June onwards Cynicus provided him with a weekly cartoon. Though it was a magazine without much political bias, the cartoons supplied by Cynicus were full of social criticism. 'Coming down from their Pedestals', the Arts humble themselves before brutish Demos. In 'Education to the Rescue' vice and intemperance try to pull back the workman whom Education is helping to climb out of the slough of ignorance.

The rich were the targets of Cynicus's scorn, yet rich art collectors rushed to buy up his work. They had spotted something they thought unrepeatable; the *Satires of Cynicus* was limited to a thousand copies, and every page was coloured by hand. Within the year the edition was almost out of print; in due course the price was doubled again, tripled, quintupled. Printsellers filled their windows with loose pages of cartoons. The unknown artist had shot to fame, as intended.

EDUCATION TO THE RESCUE.

The Satires of Cynicus

The *Satires of Cynicus* was a judicious blend of satirical, social, moral and political issues interwoven with humorous incidents. It had something for everyone. For some it reflected their own views. Reformers applauded his scorn for social hypocrisy and sham respectability. Liberals and Labour supporters approved his championing labour against capital. Bohemian circles found in him another Bohemian spirit; they loved his eccentric address and anti-Establishment stance. Others unsympathetic to his socialist leanings were impressed by his skill as an artist. Fellow-artists praised his draughtsmanship. Others simply found his sketches made them laugh.

Cynicus's cartoons were a complete novelty; yet in a way they reminded the art critics of that extinct breed of caricaturists who did not shy away from depicting vice and 'vulgar' subjects. Hence when seeking comparisons they put Cynicus on a par with Hogarth, Rowlandson and Gilray, though the most apt comparison in regard to style would have been with Daumier. What struck everyone was the force and vigour of the drawing. There was not one flabby, feeble line; all was energy and movement. Compare one of his with the traditional over-finished cartoon of the period, with its wealth of irrelevant detail and all the joke contained in the caption. Cynicus's pictures were cut down to the minimum that would tell the story without words. They delivered an instant message.

The artist is preoccupied with poverty. Have money and the world respects you, have none and it despises and shuns you. Moral judgements are based on how much you own and how smart your clothes are. 'The penny's mightier than the sword,' he quipped. 'A little earning is a dangerous thing.'

Cynicus had not received much education, but he made the best of what he had with Greek script and Latin tags. The very title has a classical ring; and the motto is from Horace: 'Sine ira et studio', without anger and partiality. The cover depicts the warrior Perseus (duly labelled in Greek) with his legendary accoutrements of polished shield and winged sandals, in the act of slaying the Gorgon, a being so hideous that all who looked on her were turned to stone. Perseus avoided that fate by looking only at her reflection in his shield. As the shield reflected the monster, so the *Satires* will reflect the vices of the age, symbolized by the Gorgon's snaky locks, inscribed Fraud, Sham, Deceit, Cant, Hypocrisy and Folly.

The satirical sketches appealed to a mood of the time. Britain was moving from having two political parties, Conservative and Liberal, towards the creation of a new political grouping—Labour. When Cynicus castigated wealth and privilege and sided with the underdog, he was expressing views that were new and gaining in popularity. In 1891 he was undeniably ahead of his time. The critics little knew just how ahead he was, considering cartoons re-used from *Quiz* were already up to ten years old.

Wednesday At Homes

The fried fish shop achieved all Cynicus wanted of it and more. Contemporaries referred to it as a 'wretched little shop', and described Drury Lane as 'that place of evil sights and smells'. An inauspicious choice, 'scarcely the way to set the Thames on fire, you will think', said Hammerton,

> but behind the Bohemian exterior of this newcomer to artistic London there lurked considerable commonsense of the shrewd Scottish variety, and presently the end had justified the means. If the Thames still ran cold beneath its bridges, "the Town" at least was agog with gossip about the remarkable work that was issuing from the studio of "Cynicus" in Drury Lane. More, the unknown artist had, on the strength of his first book of caricatures and rhymes, entitled "The Satires of Cynicus", published in 1890, become a personage of note among London's millions, and the converted fish shop was the meeting place of many of the most eminent people in London, who gathered there each week when Cynicus was "At Home".

There came reformers of all kinds, members of the Fabian Society, Social Democrats, Liberals, the founders of the Independent Labour Party, Members of Parliament, literary men and women, artists, actors, dramatists, Bohemians, journalists and newspaper publishers. The visitors remembered their host as a slight figure with alert eyes in a handsome face, a little pointed beard, and an air of mingled diffidence and self-confidence. Far from being the embittered social critic of the *Satires,* he diffused around him an atmosphere of optimism and excitement. He encouraged people to blossom. He had the knack of making friends.

Some early visitors were old friends from Dundee and Glasgow, thrilled with the wealth of theatres and concerts and exhibitions on offer. From Dundee came artists: John Duncan, Max Cowper, Alick Ritchie; the actor-producer William Mollison; and writers such as 'Norval' Scrymgeour. Fifty-nine Drury Lane became a home from home for Scots.

Some guests have left descriptions of the 'studio'. It was really just the front shop. 'Stout oak shutters and a stout front door' preserved it from the Saturday night disturbances among habitués of the taverns and the lodging house. It was inexpensively furnished. Plaids flung over

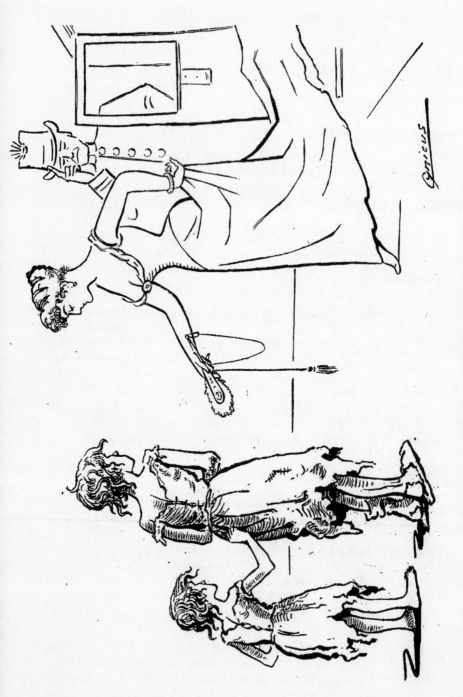

SCANTILY CLAD: BY NECESSITY AND BY CHOICE

secondhand leather chairs concealed their shabbiness, and hassocks and a cumbersome oak pew eked out the seating. Still, there was barely space for all the guests and some had to sit on the stairs. The ceiling was low, the bare floor fashionably stained black; the wainscoted walls were covered with sketches, shawls, masks and Japanese scrolls. Books were piled on shelves and a harmonium was squeezed into a corner, while in another corner a mysterious column of blacking tins grew each week taller.

The novelist Peggy Webling described those evenings in her autobiography, *Peggy:* 'Cynicus made a good host, immensely popular with all sorts and conditions of guests.' There were more men than women on those long evenings and it struck her that the guests met 'with no object but talk, even refreshments being of little account. And such talk! All about books, and plays, and pictures, and public, impersonal things, with now and again an intimacy and frankness of self-revelation which would have startled and shocked Brantford' [her Canadian home].

The evenings included entertainment, too, with guests singing, reciting poetry and playing musical instruments. The poster artist John Hassall sang student songs. William Mollison, the Dundee actor, coming from his evening performance as Rob Roy, braved stinging clouds of pipe and cigarette smoke to launch into 'Eugene Aram' or 'The Bells'. Cynicus sang comic songs, Scotch for preference, interpolated funny stories into serious discussions and ensured bonhomie. Passersby in the Lane would not have credited that the jollity within was sustained on tea and buns.

The mystery of the blacking tins was explained when on Friday nights a Drury Lane shoeblack whom Cynicus had befriended came in to present yet another tin in appreciation.

Said Cynicus:

We also entertained a King and a Princess. The King was George Ross, then known as "The King of the Cocos" ... The story went that his father, a Scots sailor, was wrecked on the Cocos, was rescued by the natives, and married the lady who was heiress to the throne. The original Ross sent his family to this country to be educated, and George came to Madras College, St Andrews, at the same time that I was a pupil there.

The Princess was Pauline Johnstone ... a poetess. She was a Mohawk Indian, head of her tribe, and I can recall an occasion when she came to the studio dressed in the full Indian dress, with a string of human teeth round her neck, moccasins, leather trousers, a tomahawk, and a dagger, and all the other accoutrements .... She recited several Indian poems on that occasion, swinging her tomahawk and flashing her dagger at the same time. And as she spoke, or rather chanted, her lines, she did so with so much spirit that it was not difficult to imagine that one's scalp stood in some danger.

Novelists of note frequented the studio—Marie Corelli, a brilliant conversationalist, and Frances Hodgson Burnett, who was interested in the Drury Lane boys club. G B Burgin, a prolific writer, perhaps introduced Cynicus to Peter Keary of the Pearson-Keary magazine empire in Henrietta Street, where Cynicus then became a daily dropper-in. Other journalists—the Barr brothers of the *Detroit Free Press,* Francis Gribble, Bart Kennedy, C N Williamson of *Black and White,* and H W Massingham of the *Star*—fraternised with the young cartoonist.

Cynicus was not overawed by his more famous guests. He had some admiration for Beatrice Potter and Sidney Webb. He was impressed by Bernard Shaw as an 'advanced thinker' and admired his abundance of energy and industry, but considered that 'showmanship was his leading quality'. (Cynicus was no mean connoisseur of showmanship.) Of William Morris, the founder of the Arts and Crafts movement, who both visited the studio and invited Cynicus to lectures at Kelmscott House: 'I found his social theories too poetical and not practical enough.'

As the Dundee journalist 'Norval' Scrimgeour recalled, 'I was introduced to Victorian novelists of worldwide reputation. But they had no swagger. Nobody was anybody in that glorified fish shop, and Martin Anderson was just the same old cheery spirit he had been in Dundee, though London was ringing with his fame.'

Politicians

Cynicus made a few real friends among politicians—William Allan MP, later Sir William, Ramsay MacDonald and Keir Hardie. They stuck by him when the fair weather friends departed.

Allan was yet another Dundonian, an older man with an exciting career behind him. At the age of twenty he had joined the Navy, was taken prisoner while blockade-running in the American Civil War, then began as foreman in a Sunderland engineering works and rose to found his own firm. His experience on the shop-floor led him first to grant his own workers an eight-hour day and then to enter Parliament as a Liberal to win it for all. Peggy Webling praised him in her autobiography as 'a burst of warm sunshine on a cold autumn day, or a strong wind on the hills'. 'His great cordial voice, his friendly smile and his air of good-fellowship made him at home on the instant. All petty and mean thoughts were swept away by his simple beneficence and faith in humanity, while his absolute self-confidence and honest pleasure in the success of his own life only made him the more lovable.' Words most of which she could have equally applied to Cynicus, had he not by then offended her.

Ramsay MacDonald came to the shop to meet the author of the *Satires,* attracted by his 'advanced views'. Cynicus was always reverential towards those he held to have advanced views, and it was balm to his spirit to be credited with them himself. The future Prime Minister, then private secretary to a radical Irish MP, was eloquent on the need for reform; he espoused the Eight-Hour Day, Old Age Pensions, Land Nationalisation, and the abolition of the House of Lords. Cynicus was bowled over by his idealism, his sincerity, his intellect. In his own eclipse he fondly remembered a time when 'Ramsay MacDonald and I walked the streets arguing our young heads off'.

Both were interested in settlement work in the East End. At Beaconsfield Mansions, a recreation centre and night refuge for destitute boys, Cynicus played the piano, MacDonald washed the stairs. At the studio MacDonald was the ladies' favourite, on account of his distinguished appearance and simple courtesy. The Webling family, unaware of his humble origins, nicknamed him The Aristocrat, as Peggy explained, 'not in any disbelief in the sincerity of his Radical outlook, rather as a compliment to his high breeding, education and handsome appearance'.

Jerome K Jerome, who had made his name in 1889 with the humorous novel *Three Men in a Boat,* had his own recollections of Ramsay MacDonald at the studio: 'He was fond of lecturing. Get him on

PUBLIC CHARITY.

" When thou doest alms, let not thy left hand know what thy right hand doeth."

the subject of Carlyle and he would talk for half-an-hour. He would stand with his hat in one hand and the door-handle in the other, and by this means always secured the last word.'

As for Keir Hardie, the Labour leader, Cynicus found him to be 'the reverse of what the Press of the day made him out to be—well read, a great Shakespeare scholar, and in his own way an intellectual man'. They had much to agree about. Both loathed the royal family, the aristocracy and the Church. Both were idealists; for that juvenile cynicism in *Quiz* cartoons had masked a streak of idealism. Both had seen severe depression in the West of Scotland coalfields, and could exchange reminiscences of hard times; but Hardie had experienced them in the wretched cottages of the miners' rows, not in cushioned Cambuslang.

Before the age of nine Hardie had been sacked from his twelve-and-a-half-hour-day, seven-day-a-week job as a baker's boy because of a crisis in his family. The drunken stepfather was out of work, the brother was gravely ill, the mother was on the point of giving birth. With three-and-six a week the child was the family's breadwinner. After some disturbed nights he was late for work. He was fired on the spot. The fact that his employer was a prosperous churchgoer put Hardie off institutional religion for good. At ten, the child went down the pit as a trapper, opening and closing a trapdoor to ensure the air supply, sitting alone in darkness.

When, in 1888, Keir Hardie vainly stood for Parliament, he received a letter of support from the London branch of the Scottish Home Rule Association, signed by the secretary, one Ramsay MacDonald. According to Cynicus, it was at the Drury Lane studio that they at last met in 1892 and set about organising the Independent Labour Party. Two campaigners for the emancipation of the working class, they had much in common, but they would go separate ways. Hardie, 'Member for the unemployed', would be an agitator, an eternal outsider, refusing to compromise; MacDonald would adapt himself to reality till he compromised his ideals.

These three powerful personalities, Allan, Hardie and MacDonald, exercised a great influence on the little artist's development. When they lectured the company on unemployment, child labour, the irresponsibility of coal owners and the need for a minimum wage of sixpence an hour he drank it all in.

He was quickly adopted into the new sphere of Labour politics. Keir Hardie's friend Frank Smith asked Cynicus for contributions to a new paper, *The Leader and Workers' Advocate,* an amalgamation of two newspapers that came into being on the 19th of September 1891 and lasted for all of three weeks. During that time Cynicus contributed three original cartoons: '"The Poor ye have always with you." No Wonder!' and two strongly anti-monarchy sketches. An editorial deplored the waste at Windsor Castle, and bemoaned the 'royal owner … punting at baccarat with a few distinguished friends … the one and only occupation that he finds congenial'. This newspaper then turned into the *Labor [sic] Leader,* 'The Organ of the Independent Labor Party', to which Cynicus contributed two cartoons a week, mostly of original material, with some pictures 'kindly lent' from the *Satires.* This commission came to an end with the newspaper's demise in December 1891.

The frank expression of radical views would prove fatal to the artist's success in London. It would also give his work permanent value.

Pride, pomp, and palaces, farewell,
I go with lowly folk to dwell.

Chapter 7—A Vagabond 1891–92

IT SEEMS LIKE an immensely busy and productive period in Cynicus's life. He was preparing to bring out a second book with forty-eight pages of illustrations and verses and twelve new full-page cartoons; he was simultaneously working for several publications; meanwhile he was taking the time to charm each new visitor that dropped into his studio, which they did at all hours.

The Humours of Cynicus

But the *Satires of Cynicus* which caused such a splash in March 1891 had been originally completed for publication by May 1890. So the second book could well have been begun in 1890, if not before. Critics were amazed that the *Humours of Cynicus* was thrown off in a few months. But far from being the work of a few months in London, it was the fruit of years of preparation in Scotland. Old *Quiz* cartoons supplied four-fifths of the smaller pictures.

Pall Mall Budget previewed the first parts of the new book a mere three months after the re-launch of the *Satires* and a couple of months before other newspapers. It, after all, held a privileged position in his heart, having printed his first ever London review and offered him his first commission.

The *Humours of Cynicus* came out in September 1891 to mainly positive reviews. The *Scotsman* hit the nail on the head when it wrote, 'It is likely to be even more popular than its predecessor, for while the drawing shows equal vigour, dexterity and simplicity, and a truly marvellous power of suggestion, we have here pure fun, and delicious humour instead of pungent satire.'

The *Globe* took issue with the *Scotsman's* review, which had enthused, 'Every picture means a fit of laughter, and those who take up the book may therefore be warned to observe moderation in turning over the pages.' 'Really?' remarked the *Globe* sourly. 'If that be so, the causes that make for laughter north of the Tweed are entirely different from those operating here. Interested and surprised at his resource and dexterity, and grieved that so clever an artist should hamper his achievement by such futile and elementary "satire" we may be in looking over the Cynicus volumes, but there is no more temptation to laugh at the drawings than there is to laugh at the caricatures of Gilray.

The Celestial Circle

LONDON:

THE CYNICUS PUBLISHING CO., 59, DRURY LANE.
AND
SIMPKIN, MARSHALL, HAMILTON, KENT & CO., LIMITED.
1892.

Earnestness rather than humour is their note. One of the best in the volumes, so far as drawing and expression goes, is the "Amor Vincit Omnes." The incident there caricatured may be untrue and even offensive, but of its power there cannot be two opinions.'—'Amor Vincit Omnes' portrays a monk and nun kissing. When Keir Hardie was editing the *Labour [sic] Leader,* he received a complaint from a Glasgow reader that a picture shown in the window of the Labour Literature Depot was 'an insult to the Catholic religion'. The picture was a Cynicus cartoon: we can guess which. Nowadays it is easy to forget that some of Cynicus's pictures were in fact 'daring', for example the elderly Prince chasing a Gaiety girl.

Despite the *Globe's* objections, the *Humours of Cynicus* was selling very well. It had a delightful cover and title-page, entitled 'The Celestial Circle', formed of Chinese children, each holding the pigtail of the one in front. The cartoons exuded an undemanding humour that everyone could enjoy, a black humour of deflated pomposity, bungles and disasters. This time Cynicus appealed to a wider public. 'Advanced thinkers' might shake their heads over social injustice and prefer the *Satires*; the public enjoyed theatre and music-hall, the farces of Pinero, the saucy repartee of Marie Lloyd and Vesta Tilley, and the *Humours of Cynicus.*

Cynicus, or more probably William, set the price at twenty-five shillings for the bound volume. The edition again consisted of a thousand hand-coloured copies, plus a hundred de luxe copies on superior paper, numbered and retouched by Cynicus at two guineas. It advertised that a few *Satires of Cynicus* could still be had, price two guineas apiece. It was a far cry from the penny and threepenny productions of 'Miss Magdalen Green'.

By the time the *Humours* was published, its creator had escaped from London and gone north.

Caravanning

During the summer Cynicus had, among everything else, found time to experience 'life on the open road'. It took him back to that exquisite sensation of waking to the sound of birdsong and the scent of greenery after a night in a Paris park. It was in noisome Drury Lane that his latest political friend suggested going off to evangelise unpoliticised countrymen. Henry Anketell was 'an Irishman... and a great Land Reformer... He used to tour the country lecturing as a disciple of Henry George and advocating the principles of the Land Nationalisation League.' The motto of the League was 'To restore the Land to the People and the People to the Land'. It campaigned against badly-built, unhealthy, crowded urban housing: lack of fresh air bred sickness, and

Amor Vincit Omnes

vile surroundings fostered drunkenness and vice. To further the cause, the Land Nationalists issued penny tracts and held van meetings throughout the country. It was no coincidence that T R Threlfall, the editor of the *Labor Leader* which employed Cynicus, was on the council; the next year Cynicus became a council member too, and subscribed an annual half guinea to the funds. He kept up his association with the Land Nationalists until he left London for good. He championed their cause for the rest of his life.

He wrote:

> I remember on one occasion, we drew into the country owned by the Duke of Bedford and took up our stance on what had formerly been the common but, due to "landlordism," had been acquired by the Duke. In his lecture that night Ankethill [*sic*] made use of the fact, and, in spite of his audience being made up mostly of servants and flunkeys from the estate, did not scruple to point out the injustice of the appropriation.
>
> Nothing happened during the meeting, but at night when we three were in our bunks in the caravan the flunkeys and servants returned, the shafts were lifted, and before we knew where we were we were being trundled at a goodish pace out of the town.
>
> At first we were considerably alarmed, but prudence kept us in our beds and we let things take their course. The next morning we awoke to find ourselves standing in a field about a mile or so from the town.

The local photographer from Ampthill immortalised the caravan. A blackboard reads, 'Meeting Tonight 7.30', and painted on the side is the slogan, 'Abolition of Landlordism. Justice for Labour'. A hand bell sits ready to attract an audience.

Another political caravanner described his experience in the *Pall Mall Budget*. He too was charmed with the peaceful flowery byways of rural England. On arriving at the meeting place he would distribute leaflets at all the cottages. If the meeting was not broken up by the landowner he attracted a large audience. To start with he entertained the labourers with comic songs. (Now we see why Anketell wanted Cynicus along.) Then he spoke. Once their interest was aroused 'they would hang about and discuss the topics among themselves'.

Caravanning was all the rage. The newspapers were full of it. Politicians, lay preachers, the Salvation Army, Home Rule campaigners, troops of actors, artists and photographers all used a caravan as touring quarters. The craze lasted into the next century, when Toad of Toad Hall was bitten by the bug. Cynicus at once became as keen as Toad. 'I purchased a vehicle which in the early days had been a lion's den with the Wombwell Circus, but had been converted by them into a living caravan.' It was small, even for a lion, and perched high on wooden waggon wheels. The interior was crammed with bunks, a chest of cooking

61

with a paraffin stove—and the Drury Lane harmonium. For years to come he got more simple pleasure out of that old van than almost any other fruit of his London success. In the end it became a source of income.

He headed for the North in his new acquisition, since Annie had been running the Tayport end of the business for months on her own.

We started very early that morning from Drury Lane and it was just breakfast time as we made to pass through Piccadilly. Unfortunately, we arrived in time to participate in a traffic jam and those who complain now of time lost in a modern version may perhaps alter their opinion of the good old days when I say that while we waited in this Piccadilly jam in the day of the cab and hansom, I not only had time to eat my porridge but cook my ham-and-eggs and eat them too. I doubt if such a scene will ever be repeated in Piccadilly.

On that trip my driver was a Yorkshireman who came of gypsy folk and he had one profitable and more or less amusing trick that he learned from the Romany folk. Regularly when we would halt on a village common, he would get out a fishing hook or line, bait the hook with a juicy worm, lower it from the caravan window to the grass and wait until a duck or chicken would happen along. It was then a case of a smart jerk and the unfortunate fowl would be in the window and despatched before any casual observer could realise what had happened. In this way and with the ever-open larder of the potato and turnip fields, we fared both economically and well.

They camped at roadsides and suffered the same treatment as gypsies and travellers, being constantly moved on by the police, until they discovered

HEREDITARY GREATNESS.

that a police summons took over a day to arrive, so that they always had time to elude prosecution.

> Throughout that first caravan tour to the North we met with the greatest kindness everywhere. For one thing we had a small organ that I kept in the van, and by its means we generally turned Saturday night in the villages into concert night.
>
> On the Sundays, too, we had the village choir, myself playing for them inside, they singing outside, and the village foregathered around. On occasion there would also be a preacher. By reason of these Saturday and Sunday affairs we rarely wanted for eggs, butter, or milk.

In this manner he gradually wended his way to Tayport. When he parked in front of the colouring studio at Grovebank, Annie's young workers clustered round the vehicle in wonder. Some patted the horse, for they were familiar with horses; a bold few ventured to peer in at the door; most were too shy to laugh at the strange little man's encouraging quips, or respond to the unintelligible gypsy's banter.

The Tayport Studio

For Annie had meanwhile trained about a dozen delicate and handicapped youngsters to colour in the plain printed outlines of Cynicus's cartoons.

> The children, at first, had no knowledge of colour whatsoever, and had to be taught everything from the beginning... I sent the sheets on from London loose, and these were distributed to each worker in bundles of six, six copies of each page. My sister would then mix, say, a pretty blue..., and beginning at the top of the first sheet, work down it, filling in everything that required a blue on the sheet. This the worker would copy on the five remaining sheets, when my sister would return and fill in on the first of the sheets again all the parts that, let us say, were to be tinted pink. And so the process went on.

It is possible to spot the work of more and less well co-ordinated hands in any copy of the Cynicus books, where sheets tinted by several workers have been bound up together. Unlike conveyor belt organisation, where a worker does one small job and never sees the finished product, Annie's system allowed each worker the satisfaction of completing a sheet.

The youngsters had been working on the *Humours*. With output growing more children could be taken on and Annie rented the Baptist Hall across the road to house them. The connection with Cynicus was to cost the Baptists dear.

Cynicus had returned to his native land crowned with glory. He at once issued invitations, beautifully and delicately painted with tiny Chinese figures on gilded boughs, to an 'At Home' in 'his studio, 31 Reform Street, Dundee'— actually the Dundee Art Club rooms. He could not fail to be pleased at a chance to show off his triumph to the stay-at-home friends. W B Lamond, C G L Phillips, Max Cowper and William Norwell were now members of the Graphic Arts Association; in a very few years Cynicus would need the Association's help to sell his pictures; a few years more and Phillips and James Douglas RSW would be enrolled among his employees; later again Norwell would bail him out when he was penniless once more. But that was all in the future. For the present he enjoyed the sprightly air and open prospects of Tayport, walked along the shore to the open sea and swatted a golf ball among the sand dunes. To friends and acquaintances he poured out a stream of anecdotes of London life. He made it sound such fun.

In the Swim

By the first of November he was back in London to relieve William, who then travelled north in his turn. Cynicus resumed his contributions to *Ariel* and *Pall Mall Budget*. The *Labor Leader* had printed his cartoons throughout his absence.

Ariel was shortlived, expiring at the beginning of February 1892, but it had helped Cynicus considerably by introducing him to many up-and-coming literary people, above all, to Jerome K Jerome. When *Ariel* failed, its staff simply moved on to Jerome's new magazine, the *Idler*, which started up in the same month. Even more enjoyable than tea with Peter Keary in the Henrietta Street office of *Pearson's Weekly* were the afternoon gatherings in Arundel Street, Strand, of the staff, contributors and friends of the *Idler*. Counteracting the formidable proprietor Jerome and the brusque editor Robert Barr, G B Burgin poured out the oil of an endless fund of funny stories, abetted by a host of others—Zangwill, Conan Doyle, Marie Corelli, E W Hornung (inventor of Raffles), Eden Philpotts, Coulson Kernahan, and the artists James Greig, Dudley Hardy and Phil May. Some of the crowd had come from *Home Chimes* and would go on to Jerome's *To-day*. They would meet again at the Vagabond Club, and at present, after tea at the *Idler* office, they could go on to Cynicus's Drury Lane At Home. He was applauded for introducing to the *Idler* teas the American Alice Livingstone; he probably also took along Peggy Webling and introduced her as a budding writer; she later landed a contract with *To-day*.

While Cynicus provided *Ariel* with political cartoons, his subjects for the *Idler* were more light-hearted and literary. All through 1892 he supplied a monthly drawing with accompanying verse. Sometimes, ominously, it was a verse with accompanying sketch—ominous because in that line his talent was often mediocre.

The *Idler* connection ensured membership of the select Vagabond Club, and a new source of influential friends. Coming to London had

certainly been the right decision. His first task for the *Idler* was to illustrate a poem by the late blind poet Philip Bourke Marston, in tribute to whom the Vagabond Club had come into being.

It was a wonderful meeting-ground for an ambitious newcomer in London. As a lover of clubs and social gatherings, Cynicus was in his element. The very aim of the club was to foster helpful contacts. 'To bring editors and contributors—men who have succeeded and men who are striving to succeed—together is one of the great aims of the "Vagabond" dinners.' The established men were supposed to help the beginners. As G B Burgin described it: 'Every member is expected to know every other member, so that a very real tie of brotherhood obtains all round.' He listed his co-Vagabonds as 'journalists, artists, faddists, misogynists, optimists, pessimists, and novelists of all descriptions'. Cynicus fits into several of the categories. Despite the high ideals of the club, Cynicus recognised that 'We were a collection of people who were interested in nothing just so much as ourselves, and found little time to study each other. Barrie was fairly constantly at the board, but had then only "When a Man's Single" to his name and was a very quiet little fellow who rarely opened his mouth and spent most of the time listening to others.' There is a touch of envy here. Barrie already had a West End success.

THE END OF THE FEAST.

Chapter 8—Reacting to Criticism 1892–94

MEANWHILE THE CYNICUS Publishing Company was flourishing. As Peggy Webling said: 'One came across them [his pictures] in all neighbourhoods, the shop in Drury Lane being his headquarters, where he put them in the window directly they were done, often dripping with gall, and now and then touched with honey.'

Symbols and Metaphors

In March 1892 the artist was working on another collection of cartoons, *Symbols and Metaphors,* which like its predecessors was coming out in parts, limited again to a thousand plus a hundred de luxe copies. An early review was useful to secure subscriptions and advance orders, so in April *Pall Mall Budget*—first again—previewed it and printed nine of the sketches from the first two parts, saying, 'Our readers are already acquainted with the style of this remarkable caricaturist, whose mordaunt humour is shown in even the slightest of his sketches.' Its remarks about the business set-up are perhaps a touch pointed: 'Mr. Anderson has given Fame some nasty knocks, but she has been very kind to him. For he is praised by the press, and his pictures are purchased by the people. And, as Mr. Anderson is his own publisher, the profits are poured into his own purse. This is an eminently satisfactory state of things. We may add that a cheap edition of the "Satires" is in the press.'

This cheap, small-size uncoloured edition of the *Satires of Cynicus* appeared in June 1892, priced at three shillings and sixpence. It offered the remaining copies of the original *Satires,* retouched and signed, at five guineas each, and it listed works in progress: *Cartoons Social and Political, Scotch Pictures, Quotations with Illustrations,* and *Lines and Outlines.* In December 1892 the companion volume, the *Humours of Cynicus,* was also published in small format at three and sixpence.

Someone was showing 'considerable commonsense of the shrewd Scottish variety', as Hammerton remarked.

Some of the cartoons in *Symbols and Metaphors* were of that powerful type that had so taken the public's fancy in the *Satires*; in that category are several redrawn and improved from *Ariel* and the *Labor Leader.*

Only a few sketches portrayed the low life subjects of the *Humours,*

such as the drink-sodden mother 'training up a child in the way it shouldn't go' so that it turns into a drunken derelict. A sketch with all his old wit shows a barber shaving a king:

Even the meanest of us may
Have some rare chance thrown in his way.

The barber casts a sly glance at the little soap-boy as he flourishes his cut-throat razor and struggles with temptation.

But mainly Cynicus struck a new tone of wistful regret. He had taken to philosophising in verse, in his *Idler* vein. Some sketches were fairly insignificant and now depended on the rhymes to give them point. There are sketches of such 'symbols' as falling leaves, falling acorns, shining stars, a hand bouncing a ball, a hand grasping at a bubble, a hand clutching a thorny rose. Some verge on the repetitive: a storm-tossed branch and a storm-tossed tree; a sketch of a sunset and one of a sunrise; an owl before a full moon, a bat before a full moon. This is not the 'mordaunt humour' promised by the early preview in *Pall Mall Budget*. Cynicus was so absorbed in composing his world-weary philosophical sentiments that he had forgotten his fame rested on vigorous drawing. Now that his sketches were required simply to serve as symbols illustrating his verse, they were pretty predictable symbols.

If this type of sketch seems tame in comparison with his earlier work, his sentiments are sometimes trite to the point of triviality. Subjected to the bonds of rhyme his thoughts too often express the self-evident. 'Fire useful is when held in check but uncontrolled the house 't will wreck.' Can self-indulgence go further? Yet nobody would quarrel with such a paradox as:

> The rock which wrecks the vessel,
> May also save the crew.

or:

> The best that's in us oft must be
> Forced out by sheer calamity.

or, accompanying the sketch of a bull with a ring in its nose:

> We follow Fashion, not because we may,
> But that it hurts to pull the other way.

There is good reason to suppose that Cynicus was reacting to criticism by proving he could rise above 'vulgar' topics. He would show them he had a pensive, serious side, in contrast to the frequently macabre humour of the *Humours of Cynicus,* with its flippant low laughs. That ubiquitous figure in the *Humours,* the man with the crumpled black suit and tile hat, has been almost supplanted by a white-haired sage in a timeless robe. Looking back to the *Satires,* we can see the sage in a walking-on part; unhappily, he has been promoted to a leading role. Happily, he is on one page pursued by that harridan from the *Humours,* who has exchanged her domestic broom for a cave-man club. Though Cynicus had abandoned *Quiz* 'vulgarity' the old fun could not be quite suppressed. The classically-attired Fame who first offered the tiresome sage a laurel wreath jumps on him when he is down—and we notice, looking back, that she had all the time been wearing hobnailed boots.

Peggy Webling wrote a *roman à clef, Felix Christie,* based on the Drury Lane studio. Her characters carp at the Cynicus figure for 'glorifying the gutter'. 'Why don't you make pictures of better subjects?' the hero asks him, and the heroine exclaims, 'It isn't genius at all. It is spurious talent. His work is cunning and ingenious, that's all. He deliberately aims low, turning his skilful hand to vulgar uses.' She condemned his sketches as 'brutal in realism, but redeemed now and again by rare touches of humour and pathos'. Cynicus, for all his surface self-confidence, was in fact suggestible. If humour and pathos were called for, he could supply them. With *Symbols and Metaphors* he turned his back on a winning formula.

He appended an epilogue:

Ye cross-grained critics who do sneer for bread,
And narrow bigots, superstition fed,
'Twas not for you, forsooth, this book was writ,
Nor has your stilted judgment shaped my wit.

But it had. The note of defiance was gone when the cheap edition of the *Humours of Cynicus* came out a few months later. There he added a self-deprecatory preface: 'Don't tell me some of the humour is poor! I could tell you that myself! You will like my later books better!' Criticism had certainly dented his confidence.

It was only in April 1893, a year after *Pall Mall Budget,* that the *Review of Reviews* eventually mentioned *Symbols and Metaphors.* The column 'New Books of the Month', which so lavished praise on his previous books, had changed its tune: 'He has much to learn before he becomes artistically pleasing.' Still, it recommended a purchase: 'There can be no doubt that Cynicus is, in his own line, the most powerful caricaturist that we have with us.'

The end of 1892 had brought forth yet another book from the Cynicus Publishing Company, the *Fatal Smile.* In a shorter form, it had been Cynicus's first contribution to the *Idler;* there it consisted of a handwritten poem with small accompanying sketches, all printed over a continuous background of angular thorny twigs; so reduced in size that it lost most of its effect. Now it had acquired extra vignettes and verse and been remade into a beautiful production. In a retouched copy the colours are bright; light and shade model every bud and berry on the twigs; shadowy imps flit about the margins. It tells the tale of a child who was bewitched by a sprite in his cradle, so that his face was fixed in a smile. In consequence his young life was blighted by misunderstandings. He smiled when his stomach was aching, and they gave him more cake. He smiled when the schoolmaster beat him, and was beaten again. He smiled at the sermon, and was branded an atheist. Hounded out of society, he died in wretchedness, and the smile on his dead face told the folk what a happy life he had led.

This was meant for Christmas, and was issued bound with red ribbon and decorated with vignettes of holly and bells. Nobody knew what to make of it. 'Some of the sketches are very droll,' the *Review of Reviews* commented wonderingly.

Of course it is an offering of Cynicus's private feelings; it has the feel of something compulsively welling up from the subconscious. He had played with the theme before. Once, in *Quiz*, a cartoon called 'Hope and Despair' reveals an agonized face behind a smiling mask. Once, in the *Satires*, a skeleton pulls up the corners of the mouth on a mask to make it smile, a conceit that reappears on the cover of the *Fatal Smile*. To his public Cynicus was always the jaunty host, the merry guest, 'the same old cheery spirit', 'the soul of good-nature'. Nobody could ever take him seriously, and he had long forgotten how to express his inmost thoughts. The fairy tale is a cry from the heart, but as always a cry disguised as a song; so disguised that no one, perhaps not even the author, realised what it was saying.

Political Crusader

It was clear, nevertheless, that something was happening. For three months in a row his regular cartoon failed to appear in the *Idler*, and when in May four were printed together, they were not what was expected. Instead of the usual literary blend of sketch and verse they were four biting political satires. Thereafter there were none.

Two of the same cartoons were also published that very month in the *Glasgow Echo,* a weekly newspaper printed by 'the Locked-out Citizen Compositors'. Its first issues had promised a weekly cartoon by 'Cynicus, the celebrated satirist of Drury Lane'. Their appearance precipitated the end of Cynicus's participation in the *Idler.* When Jerome looked back it was those cartoons that stuck in his mind. The *Echo* cartoons continued for a further seven weeks, then stopped, despite an advertisement heralding more.

The *Labor Leader,* the travels with 'Ankethill', the arguments of Ramsay MacDonald and Keir Hardie, the practical socialism of William Allan, all that had been simmering in Cynicus's shapely little head had come to the boil. His early experiences in the slums of Glasgow and Dundee returned with renewed force. He burned with sympathy for the unemployed, the exploited, the oppressed. He loathed Privilege: the legal and financial Establishments, the government, the Church, royalty, ruthless employers and landlords. To devote his talent to amusing the rich was contemptible.

He got to work devising his next book. It was to consist of cartoons social and political. He discarded his philosophical pretensions. Now he would be contentious—and hopefully the talk of the town.

The new book should somehow appeal to the moneyed collector who would pay for his own chastisement. This was a problem that the eager political crusader did not confront, for the till was still ringing. Rather than turn away custom, the Cynicus Publishing Company (in other words, William) had arranged for a new 1893 edition of the *Satires* to be printed and hand-coloured as an exact facsimile of the 1890 original.

THE SCAPE-COAT

(Cynicus conveniently forgot this later—Truth the Liar.) It also issued *Symbols and Metaphors* in a small-size cheap edition, uniform with those of the two previous books. In 1892 the Company had brought out four publications; in 1893 it ploughed the proceeds into another three.

At the start of the year Nelly had gone to Tayport and a few months later William, too, headed north. They thought things were going well for them and told a friend they were 'looking forward to extending the business as soon as they find a good chance'. Nelly spent some months in Tayport, in charge of the youngsters and glad to get a rest from Drury Lane. The overworked William had to stay much longer than arranged when he developed a fever. The friend who tells us all this was William Craigie. Then an Oxford undergraduate, he was often put up in the little flat over the shop; luckily he was built on the same diminutive scale as his hosts.

On the surface nothing had changed. There were still constant visitors to the studio, drawn by the amiable host, visits to the theatre and the D'Oyley Carte operas, social gatherings, and of course the weekly At Home, with a varied diet of music and singing, political debate, talk of plays, books and people, spiced with occasional love interest. Some marriages followed from those social evenings. Bart Kennedy, on the staff of the *Review of Reviews,* found a wife. C N Williamson, editor of *Black and White,* snapped up Alice Livingstone. Ramsay MacDonald eventually announced his engagement to Margaret Gladstone.

Yet love and marriage seemed not to apply to the Andersons. Neither Martin, Nelly nor William found a partner in this wide circle. Misinterpreting a bachelor's pleasant flirting, a rumour circulated that Cynicus had a romantic attachment to a Miss 'Marguerite' King back in Scotland. 'Marguerite' was the pseudonym used when she first exhibited in Dundee by Jessie M King, then an unknown young Glasgow artist. Craigie, as a close family friend, was able to scotch the rumour. 'I think I know Martin as well as most people and I never heard him even mention Miss King's name, which is not the usual way in such cases.' Fifteen years later, not long before her marriage to E A Taylor, she was still being invited by matchmakers to make up a tea party with Cynicus.

At first, Cynicus's bustling social life had furthered his career by bringing him into contact with all sorts of useful people. He was in the swim, to be sure, but now it was more a hindrance than a help. The problem was to find a quiet minute to get down to some creative work. Since he had always been the welcoming host with the ever-open door that was now expected of him. In June 1893 Craigie was down from Oxford and again staying at the studio. He wrote to his betrothed: 'I did very little [work] in London; there were so many visitors during the day, Max Cowper and his brother, Alec Ritchie, and William Allan, MP for Sunderland, being among them. The latter is a great character. Then we were out in the evenings on invitations and so the time went very quickly.' He probably did not realise that he was not the only one unable to get down to work for the constant interruptions. The store of *Quiz* cartoons was not quite exhausted, but frivolous humour was out. Cynicus no longer wanted to amuse. He wanted to be a serious political commentator. That meant a lot of new work.

Cartoons Social and Political

In October 1893 Cynicus set off for Tayport. As usual this signalled that he had one more book finished and in the shop-window. *Cartoons Social and Political* was the fifth, and destined to be the last, large, expensive, hand-coloured edition. He had reverted to lashing the Establishment—monarchy, Parliament, clergy, lawyers, financiers and journalists. The public that expected small comic sketches, to raise a smile between lashes, was disappointed. Instead, they found thirty-six full-page plates of denunciation.

He re-used the *Glasgow Echo* cartoons that lost him the *Idler* commission, as well as some early cartoons that had already appeared in *Ariel* and the *Labor Leader.* It had always been his thrifty policy to keep the copyrights and recycle the drawings.

The new cartoons are striking and powerful, a hundred years later they still apply; but the whimsical fun has evaporated; some do not raise even a wry smile. The *Satires* encouraged warm feelings of sympathy for the poor, *Cartoons Social and Political* accuses their oppressors. This book, with its moral tone and obvious political bias, appealed to a much narrower audience.

In November the *Glasgow Herald* review said: 'Such a volume as this has no rival or competitor... The wit of this volume is as clever as the drawing. Cynicus's books should be prized in the present, and will certainly be very valuable to his abhorred rich man in the future.' The *Review of Reviews* commented briefly the next January: 'Cynicus continues to lash the social and political follies and sins of his time with the satire of his pencil. His work is as broad as ever and as forcible. Certainly there is no living cartoonist more able to preach a moment's sermon: his drawings are almost brutal in their directness.' But there were no art notices, no acclaim, no stream of eager buyers.

Other journals that had praised him in the past were silent. Had Cynicus misjudged his public? Had he been carried away by the approval of his progressive friends? He readily fell in with other people's views. Thus he had laid aside vulgarity and become anodyne for much of

JOURNALISM

Gloating in gore and gruesome gabble
A palfry pimp who panders to the rabble.

Symbols and Metaphors. Thus he now thought of himself as a political crusader. His new book's reception surprised and angered him. It did not dawn on him at once that he had gone too far and estranged the public; but gradually it became apparent that the cartoon-buying classes were not going to hang these prints in their homes, offices and clubs as he suggested, and risk offending their own clients.

Truth the Lyre

An interview published in the *Sketch* in March 1894 affords a rare glimpse of Cynicus the conversationalist. It is illustrated by Alick P F Ritchie's portrait of the artist's handsome head with its straight nose, neat pointed beard and moustaches. As Cynicus and his brother and sister gave tea to a bunch of afternoon At Home callers in Drury Lane we can see the interviewer succumbing to the atmosphere and falling a new conquest to Cynicus's charm, terming him 'a young Scotsman' when he was turning forty.

'I imagine,' began the interviewer, 'a lot of kindly and some critical people look in on Cynicus in his artist's quarters?'

'Oh! dear me, yes. All sorts of reformers and people with every imaginable crank and fad come here. I meant to tell you some of them, but, seeing how I put my last sentence, I had better not. Don't utter it! It's in your face. You want to ask why the faddists and the cranks come. To be candid, I suppose it's because they expect to find a brother.'

Cynicus pulled the wool over the interviewer's eyes by claiming to have been studying art in London before he joined the *Dundee Advertiser.* Asked why he came to Drury Lane, he explained: 'It was cheap to come here, and I wanted to feel I was in the very heart of the great human turn-about of London. Why, I have only to take a little stroll, and notions which find their way into my notebooks present themselves on every hand. You cannot help getting colour into you if you live where it is splashed the thickest... If I had been rich and gone to live and work in the suburbs, I should never have done anything but be rich and in the suburbs—which might, though, have had its advantages.'

Yet the truth is that he had already moved to the suburbs. Clearly, if there were afternoon At Homes and evening At Homes, there was little time left to prepare new drawings. A move to quieter surroundings might lend itself to new inspiration. Any surroundings would be quieter at that period. In November the *Globe* was to make the state of Drury Lane the topic of a front page article. If the reader 'does not go soon, there will be nothing much left worth his looking at, for already there is a sorry yawning gap on the west side, where its mystery was thickest, and a long stretch of the old Lane's most characteristic houses has disappeared, with nothing now to mark their place but the too familiar and depressing prospect of broken bricks and dead cats, enclosed by a grimy hoarding'.

The constant noise and dirt of demolition work all around the artist's studio was scarcely conducive to creativity. With memories of the green lawns and peace of Richmond, where he had earned five pounds so many years ago, he adjured William to find a house for them near Richmond Park. They could afford it, he said. William took a lease of 20 Eleanor Grove in Barnes, just as they were unable to afford it.

Cynicus should have heeded the wisdom of his own words: 'If I had been rich and had gone to live and work in the suburbs, I should never have done anything but be rich and in the suburbs.' For now that he had moved to the suburbs, that hoped-for new burst of creativity did not materialise.

'I am about to draw upon my note-books for a series of social satires I am contemplating, for another volume of social and political cartoons, and for other ventures that I have in mind.' This, like earlier and later much-heralded streams of forthcoming publications, did not come forth.

THE PURSUIT OF PLEASURE.

Chapter 9—Debacle 1894–98

When Funds Are Low

IN OCTOBER 1894 Cynicus escaped to Tayport as usual. He found his aunt Ann Martin and his sisters Marion and Lizzie financially in a bad way. When William Martin died in 1855 his estate, consisting of a good number of residential properties, mostly in Tayport, had been mortgaged to the local building society for five hundred pounds. Over the years the family had mortgaged their inheritance for further sums, some to enable Mrs Anderson to set up in Cambuslang. The building society allowed them to sell one of the houses in 1894, reducing the amount of security available to cover their mortgage, but they were progressively falling further and further behind with paying the interest. Cynicus, unaware that his London triumph was over, bought Grovebank, the house where the colouring operations were based, where Annie lived, and to which he, William and Nelly were constantly returning, and thus disposed of his ready cash just when it was becoming difficult to earn any.

In 1894 there was no new batch of publications from the Cynicus Publishing Company in London. Only towards the end of that year did a small, cheap compilation of pictures from previous books appear, priced at one shilling. *Cynicus His Humour and Satire* had a hand-coloured cover but was otherwise uncoloured. As if to prove he was not devoid of new ideas, several pages were devoted to giving samples of cartoons from forthcoming books, from which we see he intended to re-use *Quiz*, *Idler* and *Ariel* material. Significantly his next book would be purely humorous. He, or William, had realised the mistake. Four collections were said to be either 'Nearly ready', 'In preparation' or 'In progress'. This was all bravado, as Cynicus needed to elicit subscribers' down-payments to enable him to get one book into print, far less four. He failed to whet their appetites and not one of the four books ever appeared.

The previous year Craigie had been asked to dig up 'a number of poetical extracts for him to make designs for'. The book that was 'Nearly ready' was entitled *Quotations with Illustrations*. But sketches were never wasted; they would appear years later as prints and postcards.

In 1894 a large number of Cynicus's original paintings were sent for sale to the Graphic Arts Association in Dundee. That city was the best place in Scotland to exhibit when wealthy local businessmen like Bell, Duncan and Orchar were building up their collections. The Dundee collectors might not know that Cynicus was going out of fashion in the South. In fact, he sold ten cartoon originals at between five and ten pounds each and a painting called 'The Rising of the Moon' for the remarkable price of £52.10s. It was a very necessary boost to the funds.

In London, Cynicus prints were still to be seen in printsellers' windows and the various editions of his books still sold, but the rush had passed. Perhaps he was to some extent a victim of his own success, in that his pictures and his distinctive style had become so well known that their initial startling novelty was lost. Also, he had joined 'advanced thinkers' of the Left and lost the feel of the times. Gilbert and Sullivan were heavy enough intellectual fodder for the art-loving classes of the Nineties. He too adored the Savoy operas and knew all the ditties by heart. They could have provided so many quotations to illustrate, but he had taken to keeping fun and work in separate compartments.

So he had tied up his money by purchasing the Tayport house, while the Cynicus Publishing Company was still waiting to recoup the amount that went into producing his last book. The blockmaker, the paper supplier and the colourman, the printer, the binder and the colourists in Tayport, all had to be paid, but *Cartoons Social and Political* was not selling nearly as well as the previous books. There was never to be a call for a small-size cheap edition to match the earlier three.

While Cynicus was absent in Scotland William, besieged by creditors, mentioned the problem to Peter Keary, now the wealthy owner of many weekly papers. Their old friend at once offered a loan of a hundred pounds to tide them over. William accepted. So began a long unpleasantness.

Not a word of this worry appeared in Cynicus's memoirs. Characteristically he seized instead on a fillip to his ego that had absurdly cheered his drooping spirits. While in Tayport he was invited to Glasgow by 'Drooko' Wright, the umbrella-maker, along with the actor William Mollison, to the opening of new premises. Cynicus approved of Wright's belief in advertising, and considered him to be 'in many respects well ahead of his time in this modern essential in salesmanship'. Cynicus knew all about salesmanship, if not about cash-flow. And he certainly was an expert on umbrellas; they were an indispensable adjunct to the population of his sketches.

Wright was so tickled by an umbrella skit in the *Humours* that he wanted Cynicus to draw him an advertisement. At the studio Wright met Peggy Webling's young sister Lucy, the actress who played Little Lord Fauntleroy in Mrs Hodgson Burnett's play. 'Drooko' stipulated that she must be the model. The sketch appeared in September's *Bailie*.

The umbrella verse, originally in *Quiz,* was used yet again nine years later to advertise a different umbrella-maker. Nothing wasted.

Back to Penny Pamphlets

Now that he had given up producing comic sketches and saw himself in the role of serious social critic, he willingly consented to illustrate political pamphlets. Unfortunately they offered little financial reward. Typical is an 1895 tract 'Subjection with Charity versus Freedom with Justice', costing one penny and 'not written for profit', while the cartoon was used 'by kind permission' of its creator.

In June 1895, two Cynicus cartoons were featured on the front page of the *Weekly Times & Echo,* 'A Liberal Newspaper of Political and Social Progress'. Keir Hardie sold a pamphlet of Cynicus cartoons for a penny in the offices of the *Labour Leader.* Such work might keep up the artist's reputation in progressive circles but would not keep him, William and Nelly afloat for long in London. During the General Election, 'The only time he is considered!' with a Liberal and a Conservative candidate on their knees before a worker, each imploring his vote, could be had as a hand-coloured cartoon from the Cynicus Publishing Company, 59 Drury Lane, for a penny.

Then the *Weekly Times & Echo* commissioned Cynicus to do precisely what he had held out against: every week he was to illustrate some topical occurrence and caricature Salisbury and Chamberlain. But by now he must have been grateful for any assignment. When he had duly drawn topical cartoons for some weeks, the paper started to print his comic cartoons as well, limericks and sketches in the *Quiz* spirit of wet accidents and disastrous courtships. This source of income stopped in November. The newspaper cartoons were to come out in pamphlet form, but never got beyond the 'In Preparation' stage.

More political pamphlets followed, such as 'The Blue Button, or Temperance Spouters as Landlords' Touters' and 'The Curse of Landlordism and How to remove it' for the Land Nationalisation Society. Cynicus remained on the General Council of the LNS until he left London, still paying a generous annual subscription he could ill afford.

In the spring of 1896 the *Idler* accepted a short article for a series on 'the most beautiful woman in the world'. Cynicus chose the former actress Mary Anderson, Barrie's favourite too. Peggy Webling said she was 'like the most beautiful marble statue'. When one thinks of Cynicus's predilection for statuesque female embodiments of Justice,

The Last Hope of the Land-starved Labourer

Fame, Nobility, and so on—ideal, not realistic representations of womanhood—one understands his choice. This was the only article Jerome took from his former friend.

Cynicus could not but notice the gradual change from praising his work to finding fault. For the *Review of Reviews,* when last it mentioned him, termed him 'a forcible if not very artistic caricaturist'. His humour was heavy, his satire weak, his cartoons mere platitudes in print, decided another reviewer. His drawing was belatedly discovered to be crude, his subjects vulgar. Fame stamped on him with her hobnailed boots.

The Angel of Civilisation

Cold-Shouldered

Once the trend had set in, it continued till the outsider was frozen out. Those who once fêted him lost interest. He had become mildly ridiculous. His attempts to scintillate laid him open to scorn. 'Cynicus was the most sincere admirer and discriminating critic of his own work, being quietly, happily and delightfully self-satisfied,' wrote Peggy

Webling. 'I saw a room in the house of one of the Andersons' friends hung with his original drawings, and he made little remarks about them as we walked round, just as if they had been drawn by somebody else: "That's very scathing, isn't it?—I *do* like this one—rather vulgar perhaps—good again—most humorous—" and so on.' (This scene also appeared in *Felix Christie*.)

G B Burgin, too, mocked the little man's self-conceit:

"Cynicus" was the soul of good-nature, and on hearing of my approaching marriage confided to me that he was going to present me with a really great picture which he proposed to paint for that memorable occasion. From time to time he dropped in to tell me how the picture was getting on, and at length took me to his studio in Drury Lane… "It's a picture of a chamois on its native mountain top," he explained, as he proudly drew aside the curtain which hid this great work from the vulgar gaze. The body may have been that of a chamois, but the horns were the antlers of a public-house signboard stag.

On another occasion he confided to me that he had two wealthy old aunts in England who had never taken the slightest notice of him. One day he found himself in the village where they lived, and saw them coming toward him in an open carriage drawn by a pair of fat horses. "And I said to myself," he continued, "When I was poor and unknown these women took no notice of me. Now that I am really great, shall I show my magnanimity by bowing to them, or shall I not? I cut them dead."

Martin Anderson not only lost fair weather friends; he offended others by insensitive remarks. Along with his gift for making friends he had the faculty of putting their backs up. He could never resist a witticism, even if it would offend. He never understood that others might be as sensitive as himself.

James Greig, an Arbroathian of humble origin who became art critic for the *Morning Post*, objected forty years later to his origins being revealed in Cynicus's memoirs. '"Idler" people, Barr, Jerome and Burgin,' Cynicus wrote, 'were so taken with his promise they collected enough to send him to Paris to study, where through his characteristic industry and application he became a leading authority on the Old Masters.' Greig was not mollified by the appreciation of his talents; he was stung by the revelation that he had started as a newspaper boy, and wrote an angry letter to the paper denying everything

At some point Cynicus wounded Peggy Webling, too. She had begun to write stories when they first met. He gave her his counsel: 'It was advice in keeping with his name. "All you have to do, Miss Peggy," said he in his pleasant, soft Scots voice, "is to be brilliant, brief, witty and original".' Evidently, she charmed Cynicus and he charmed her. But he was fond of her in his own sexless way, while she expected to progress to a closer relationship. In her autobiography *Peggy* she romanced: 'He is a bachelor. I rather fancy he would have echoed a reason attributed to Lord Leighton for not marrying: "If I did, it would make one happy, but break too many other hearts".' She made the hero of *Virginia Perfect* (1909) an uneasy combination of an undersized cartoonist from Drury Lane and a sculptor friend who died. The heroine demurs at the vulgarity of his low-life sketches, and he agrees: 'All I do is glorify the gutter.' At the end he weds the heroine.

Everyone who read her novel *Felix Christie,* however, got her revised estimate of Cynicus. Peggy wrote her novels out of her journal, sometimes verbatim. *Felix Christie* gives us a snapshot of Cynicus at the crisis in his affairs. 'All his movements were quick and hurried, and he spoke quickly, his words tumbling over one another. He was thin and pale,… his figure spare and below middle height; he was too narrow in the chest, but neither insignificant nor mean in appearance, for he held himself well, making the most of his inches.' Perceptively, she has him 'dancing like a butterfly in the sunshine, or dragging his weary feet through the clods of the valley of despair'. She saw behind the cheerful mask.

By 1896 the Andersons had relinquished their suburban villa in Barnes and were back near Drury Lane, at 24 Brunswick Street. Things were turning sour.

Should auld acquaintance be forgot,
And never brought to mind?
Yes, when he has a shabby coat,
And Fortune's been unkind. (*Satires of Cynicus*)

In 1896, apart from penny tracts and one or two paragraphs in the *Idler,* one searches in vain for examples of his work in the myriad illustrated publications. What had happened to all his publishing friends and acquaintances? Could they not help him out with a small commission or print a cartoon somewhere? Apparently not. Cynicus was, of course, not without his pride and most likely concealed the true state of affairs from chance acquaintances, but what about the bosom friends? He did in fact swallow his pride and send unsolicited cartoons to Peter Keary, whom he still owed for the hundred pound loan. It was to no avail; they were not published, not even returned.

Cynicus cherished his rancour for thirty-six years and devoted an entire instalment of his memoirs to Keary. On the face of it, it is an appreciative account of the magazine proprietor's rise to riches. Keary and Arthur Pearson were so successful at editing Newnes' paper *Tit-Bits* that they went into business themselves and set up a rival paper, *Pearson's Weekly*.

> Keary, when I knew him first, was living in the poorer quarter of Islington; … when the paper was fairly launched on the wide sea of success he moved to Wimbledon. I was invited to the house warming, and found the new home a palatial place. After dinner, Keary conducted me to the billiard-room. Its walls were hung with paintings and included one… for which he had paid five hundred guineas. He had a winding staircase in the house which… he had covered with a specially manufactured carpet which… cost several hundreds of pounds. In the billiard room was also a whole orchestrina, a mechanically-driven robot band… which he had specially imported from Germany at a cost of some thousands…Keary that night boasted that fine as his house was, he would have an even better one before he was done.

Is this ingenuous admiration or the subtle exposure of a vulgarian? Keary's widow evidently thought the latter, and wrote an angry letter.

In 1903 a column from the *Morning Post* was sent to Dundee and reprinted in the *Dundee Advertiser*. It suppurates with a mixture of envy and malice. While overtly congratulating Cynicus on his second career, there is hardly a sentence but contains a poisoned barb. 'Uninformed editors offered him commissions, and hasty critics, ever on the hunt for something new, hailed him as a genius—a new Rowlandson… Critics and editors, however, found out the mistake they had made.'

Was that the only reason London dropped him? Was there something else deeply buried by time?

With Wealth it matters not how vile you be ;
The world forgives all sin but Poverty.

Chapter 10—Starting Again 1898–1902

NEEDLESS TO SAY, Cynicus swallowed his own smoke. No word of this disastrous turn of events appears anywhere in the memoirs. There he maintains that the increasing volume of business obliged him to be present in Tayport. But he probably thought that, rather than remain at a loose end in London, he might as well be on the spot helping Annie. She had been keeping her workforce busy with local orders for calendars, invitations, programmes, menus and greetings cards. Her business might be without artistic pretensions, but it was viable. Cynicus was amused to discover they were making money for a London firm. This firm cannibalised old books for prints, sent them to Annie for colouring, then glued them to panels and varnished them over to produce instant 'antiques'. They sold extremely well. He was reminded of the 'Old Masters' certain impecunious artists had turned out for London fakers in their hungry days.

Prints were now the prestige end of the business. Though there were no new cartoon collections to colour, sets of prints were still popular; and the market was growing for hand-painted humorous greetings cards.

We have more than one description of the Tayport factory and its employees at this period. Susan left school in 1896 at the age of eleven and was taken on after her twelfth birthday as the youngest colourist. She worked from nine to five on weekdays with an hour off for lunch, and from nine to one on Saturdays. For a thirty-nine hour week her wage was two shillings with a daily glass of milk and two weeks annual paid holiday.

This was quite a decent wage for the time, bearing in mind that she had first to be trained. Little maidservants commonly got no cash wages. Training and a midday meal were considered reward enough for the physical labour of scrubbing floors and carrying coal and water, and the unpleasantness of dealing with the employers' slops and laundry. By comparison the work for Cynicus was easy. But when Annie scolded her for spoiling a print, Susan took her holiday pay and left.

Cynicus found himself once again fertile in ideas. New subjects presented themselves. Hapless clergymen on the golf course furnished golfing puns and illustrated quotations from the poets. Children provided gentle humour. 'The Modern Woman' is a comely person who ignores her suitor's proposal in favour of studying dynamics. At home,

E·man cipated !

while the baby falls out of its cradle and the cat, making off with the fish, tips a jug over it, the female devotee of 'Modern Culture' reads political economy. On the road, 'The Coming Woman', an academic cyclist attired

Dearest

As it will take me all my time to get the past I

[Blum & Degen]

in vast knickerbockers and smoking a pipe, is only less horrible than the next stage, 'E-*man*-cipated', who has cut her hair, adopted male attire, monocle and cigarette, and carries golf clubs.

Away from the backbiting of London now, in the village where he was a great man and the object of the children's veneration, Cynicus felt reinvigorated. With remarkable buoyancy he shook off dejection, rediscovered his love of golf, organised the workers to produce an operetta, promised an all-day picnic when summer came, and in the course of bracing walks along the seashore planned to expand the business.

It was lucky the little man had a sunny nature. His life-long motto was 'The best is now. The best is yet to be.' So he allowed no regrets to tarnish his enthusiasm. If noble political themes were not wanted at present they could wait. In the meantime he must pocket any ambition to be a serious cartoonist.

As soon as he was reconciled to this, fate quite literally dealt him a winning card. Only it took him some time to realise it.

In 1894 the British Post Office had reluctantly allowed Britain to join Germany, Austria and France in the private manufacture of postcards. Since the Post Office insisted that the whole of one side must be kept free for the address, as on an envelope, the first postcards bore just a small view on the other side, with space for a message. Like many other postcard publishers, Messrs Blum & Degen started with views, vignettes of town scenes; but in 1898 they brought out something refreshingly different, three sets of comic sketches. These at once sold out and were reprinted.

Though the designs were all new, former subscribers to *Quiz* might have recognised the style. The usual space for a message was not entirely blank but showed the beginning of a stilted letter of excuse. Alongside, a small sketch revealed the real trouble. 'Having some urgent business to attend to...' meant mending his trousers; 'Having been very busily engaged at home...' meant punching his wife; 'As I am very reluctantly compelled to keep the house...' because the wife, brandishing the tongs, barred his exit. 'I trust you will forgive my strong attachment' is penned by our old *Quiz* character hanging by his coat tails. In need of cash Cynicus had lowered his sights, and found, though he still did not know it, the pot of gold.

Ten years earlier the enterprising spirit had not taken long to reflect, Why work for a publisher? Why not be one's own publisher?

His fine sixteen-page advertising booklet of 1900, *Cynicus His Art and Work,* made no mention of postcards. The covers advertised magic lantern slides for sale or hire, and touted *Cynicus His Humour and Satire* and the *Fatal Smile.* 'The colourists, presided over by Cynicus himself, work together in a large, bright, airy studio.' A photograph showed them posed in the garden of The Grove, as the house was now called, twenty-six young folk, the girls in white aprons and sleeves, with long hair down their backs, Cynicus standing at an easel to one side, and a sister working at a table on the other. The booklet described the 'quaint and old-fashioned' process of producing coloured prints, even the colours being ground by hand. Beginning with the artist's soft-outline drawing, the copyists, according to their grade of training and talent, applied the first tints, the second tints, the third and fourth as required. Modelling was obtained by overpainting with deeper tones. Cynicus himself put in the finishing touches and finally signed the picture. 'Ere the pictures have reached this stage, they have passed through the different artists' hands from twenty to thirty times, and in the larger subjects from forty to fifty times.'

Later pages listed his four published albums and appealed for subscribers for his forthcoming book, *Lines and Outlines,* which promised to be 'an entirely new line of thought, not shewn in his other works'.

One hundred and thirty-four Humorous and Satirical prints were offered at a shilling each; eight large panels at half a crown; and thirty

Cartoons Social and Political at sixpence. (He must have brought stacks of unsold copies back from London.) In addition, the company could supply humorous birthday cards, Christmas and Valentine cards, and 'sympathy' cards; a hundred and forty designs in all, as well as albums, menus and programmes; it undertook coloured maps, armorials, illuminated addresses, wall decorations and friezes; and would frame prints on the premises.

This expensive free booklet was sent out in the usual openhanded Cynicus manner. He was conceding that what made a profit was the comic stuff he used to dismiss. But still he did not realise what was before his nose.

When accommodation for the colourists again became cramped he bought a photographer's old glass studio and re-erected it in the garden. 'When I arrived in my caravan I was able to drive through the big gateway and draw up practically alongside the studio. We then used the caravan for an office.'

Cynicus was in love with the simple life. He often toured rural Fife in the caravan, leisurely retouching one of his works to turn it into a de luxe copy. He liked to park near friends for an impromptu social evening, and local children congregated at the caravan wherever it went. Sometimes it would be seen on the sands of Tentsmuir. Sometimes in remote corners it served as a chapel for an evening service, with the farm folk gathered round singing to the strains of the harmonium within. Like its owner, it was to enjoy a second career at Castle Cynicus.

Freed from the struggle to keep afloat in London, suppressing the memory of unpleasant episodes, giving himself up to simple pleasures, Cynicus managed to be happy. Looking back on the London years, he could congratulate himself. Unknown, an outsider, the cartoonist had splendidly conquered the metropolis and forced it to acknowledge his talent. He had succeeded on the social level too, been host and guest of notables, a compeer of leading journalists and a 'Vagabond'. On the personal side he had enjoyed stimulating gatherings with kindred spirits, and provided a livelihood for William and Nelly, Annie and a band of poor Fife children.

From the London end things looked different. Though the shop-sign emblazoned 'Cynicus Publishing Company' had remained above 59 Drury Lane for a year or two after he left London, the shop that had seen so many famous visitors, so many jolly At Homes, was now generally closed. When Cynicus left them in the lurch, as they felt, after pouring out on them his resentment at London's change of heart, William and Nelly kept the shop going as best they could, letting the flat to a newsagent and lodging nearby in Great Ormond Street, till in 1900 the

[Courtesy of N.E. Fife District Museum Service]

newsagent took over the shop as well. Still smarting from his young brother's censure, William had determined to look after Nelly instead, and washed his hands of the Cynicus Publishing Company.

Martin considered William had betrayed him and never forgave him for accepting the loan from Keary; and Keary, it seems, was not averse to reminding him of it. He blamed William moreover for neglecting the shop. Keir Hardie had come to see about pamphlets and found it closed. William kept silence, but he was deeply hurt when his younger brother assumed the mantle of Mother and vented righteous wrath. After all, he and Nelly could not live on nothing. He had the bills to pay. He had given up his career to further Martin's, but he was not without his own talent, and he had taken a job. It was hard to be blamed for the inevitable.

On 7 June 1902 Nelly married a fellow lodger, a forty-year-old widower journalist called Loxton Hunter. Nelly was forty-seven but gave her age as forty-two. Martin was not the only Anderson who looked less than his years.

When a *Sunday Mail* reporter interviewed Cynicus in 1929 and asked why he left London, he sensed an evasion in the artist's reply: 'He looked up as though to peer through the window. "I was country bred

and I wanted to be back in Scotland".' After thirty years it was still too painful for him to admit the truth. But a private letter written in 1904 to Keary acknowledged that he had 'had to struggle with misfortune and adversity'.

Cynicus left London in 1898. Did he miss it? Of course he did. He missed the mutual sharpening of wits. He was appalled at the self-satisfaction of the closed minds that made up Tayport society. Three churches in Tayport and five in Newport, all at loggerheads, ministered to the spiritual wellbeing of the district, without obvious success. Religion was for Sunday and Sunday was for religion. Blinds were pulled down, toys put away, singing and whistling forbidden. In funereal black the citizens walked to church, Bible and hymnbook well displayed, peppermints hidden in the pocket, and walked back two hours later anticipating their substantial luncheon. Tradesmen became elders to promote their business and had to give the clergyman indefinite credit. Cynicus found unchanged the very village he had lampooned in *Miss Magdalen Green's Grand Tour.*

A Town Councillor

He got himself elected to the Town Council. Tayport Town Council was a self-willed oligarchy, and sometimes a dictatorship. 'To even up marshy bits', the council said, it had directed the refuse collectors to dump their noisome loads, including the contents of the citizens' earth closets, on the public common. Complaints—and there were many—were ignored. When the Volunteers proposed a new shooting range across a public road the provost expected the council to rubber-stamp his private arrangement with the local landlord. He found Cynicus an exasperating rebel.

After a year Councillor Anderson called a public meeting. Tayport was agog. His old employer, the *Dundee Advertiser,* sent either a phlegmatic or a deaf reporter, who wrote briefly 'Although interruptions were frequent during the course of the lecture, the proceedings were on the whole of a good-natured description.' The man from the *Courier,* on the other hand, attended a sensational meeting where the audience almost came to blows.

Ever since Mr Anderson announced that he was to speak on his first year's experiences as a Town Councillor in Tayport the greatest excitement prevailed, and last night it was feared that nothing short of a riot would occur. With a view to preventing this, a large staff of constables was in the vicinity, but fortunately, although at times the shouting and yelling was terrific, their services were not required. Throughout the whole meeting a great noise prevailed, and never a minute passed but the speaker was interrupted by shouting and singing. At several stages some of those present, members of the opposition, caused great anger on the part of the majority of those present, and it would not have taken much more to begin a free fight amongst a section of the men. The lantern slides shown caused the greater part of the disturbance.

Mr Anderson went into detail regarding the question of the Commons, and other matters of interest to the ratepayers, but scarcely a minute passed without serious interruptions. A considerable number of those present apparently attended for the purpose of causing disturbance, and on several occasions it seemed as if several of these excited persons would be ejected. They started numerous songs, but their efforts were drowned by the angry expostulations of the majority, and cries of "Shut up!" and "Throw them out!" were frequent.

Needless to say, the lantern slides were comic cartoons.

Cynicus changed the title of his print, 'A Peace Meeting', which showed a group of men in heated argument, into 'The Town Council'. He attended the Town Council meetings conscientiously till November 1902. Only one series of conclaves he pointedly avoided—those devoted to deliberating on how best to show loyal grief at the death of Queen Victoria. The Council was greatly relieved when he became so engrossed in other projects that he did not stand for re-election. A new enthusiasm was absorbing a great deal of his time and taking him the five miles to and fro between Tayport and Balmullo.

A Peace Meeting

Chapter 11—The Company and the Castle 1902–04

BEFORE THE START of 1902 Cynicus had reluctantly been convinced that postcards were the coming thing. He later disclaimed having thought of it for himself.

It was forced upon me. The fact that my sketches were peculiarly suitable for the postcard was set before me, and I was in the fortunate position of having retained all my copyrights, so that I had plenty of material to hand over when a company was formed to carry out the idea.

But there was one insuperable obstacle. Tayport could not print in colour. They could produce postcards to be painted by hand but not the colour-printed copies that sold so briskly.

John Allan, son of Annie's commercial traveller and as enthusiastic and imaginative, as charming and persuasive as Cynicus himself, was probably the one who forced it upon him. On the 3rd of March 1902 the Cynicus Publishing Company was incorporated as a limited company, with issued capital of £3,000 subscribed by one of the seven shareholders, a substantial Dundee draper named Archibald Lawson, to finance colour printing on the premises. The other six shareholders were John Allan, as the company's commercial traveller; their printer R A Hardie; Cynicus, Annie and younger brother John; and their Glasgow lawyer, R Yorston. All the males except John were appointed directors. Cynicus contributed the business and all his copyrights, with The Grove, in exchange for £1,500 in cash and £6,000 in shares, with a salary of £3 a week for the next ten years. Allan sold his stationery and fine art business to the firm for £1,000 in shares. Hardie sold his machinery and stock for £500 worth. Cynicus allotted his 6,000 shares thus: 4,500 to himself; 500 to Yorston; and 500 each to Annie and John. Was it to justify John's living in The Grove with the director and manageress that he was designated 'artist' before dropping out of sight again, next to appear as 'retired'? John is elusive.

They were all set to go. In May the company submitted plans for premises to be erected alongside The Grove. This was built at a cost of £2,500. By October they already needed to extend. Colour printing presses were installed upstairs, 'and the foremost colour-printer in the country brought from Edinburgh'.

They were now ready to use the three-colour printing process to fill in the outlines. Three photographic negatives were made and from them three half-tone process blocks were engraved. These were printed in yellow, red and blue, so that mixtures of the three colours reproduced all the intermediate tones of the original painting. The company's first colour-printed postcards were circulating by the second half of 1902.

Postcards at Last

Since his early newspaper work had trained him to make a point in small room, Cynicus was not cramped by the vignette format that had been imposed on British manufacturers. He drew a minister in painful contact with a golfer's club; a holidaymaker on the nightly hunt for small game in his bed; fashionably, a cyclist ricochetting from a close encounter with a pedestrian; traditionally, a drunk supporting himself along railings ('Proceeding by Rail'). From earlier days he repeated some old favourites: 'The Band of Hope' fishing from Broughty pier; the drunken 'Venus' vociferating from the police stretcher; the married couple quarrelling 'At Home' and all sweetness 'Abroad'; the brawling family of 'Home Sweet Home'. All these he had ready as prints.

For the Scottish market he misapplied six Burns quotations, perhaps those suggested by William Craigie. The best of them was a greatly improved version of 'Turn Again, Thou Fair Eliza' from *Quiz*; now it is a small hot manic figure that turns the mangle.

The sentimental customer had to make do with the children of the *Humours of Cynicus,* gawping at the hat-shop window, agonising outside the dentist's, enjoying a turnip, being defeated by a plum-pudding or a pie. In this set was the popular 'Her First Bawl', a howling baby.

Bearing in mind that many purchasers had difficulty with writing and would find it hard to fill up half a side of the card, he repositioned the pictures in his next Scottish set to leave just space for a short greeting or signature at the base. The winner here was 'Much Ado About Nothing', a close group of gossips in mutches. It was used again and again for years to come to convey all sorts of gossip, from sectarian controversy to wartime propaganda, and was eventually taken over by the postcard publishers Messrs Tuck.

In 1902 came an important development. The Post Office at last allowed postcards to bear the address on half of one side, with the message on the other half. This freed the whole front of the postcard for a picture. It was like a starting gun. Suddenly, postcards were all the rage. All who could afford it began collecting cards, filling albums, sending scores of cards which bore as sole message 'Send me cards!' A characteristic sight of early twentieth century holidays was people hovering round postcard displays at the stationers', sitting down with sheaves of postcards, painfully cogitating messages, licking stamps.

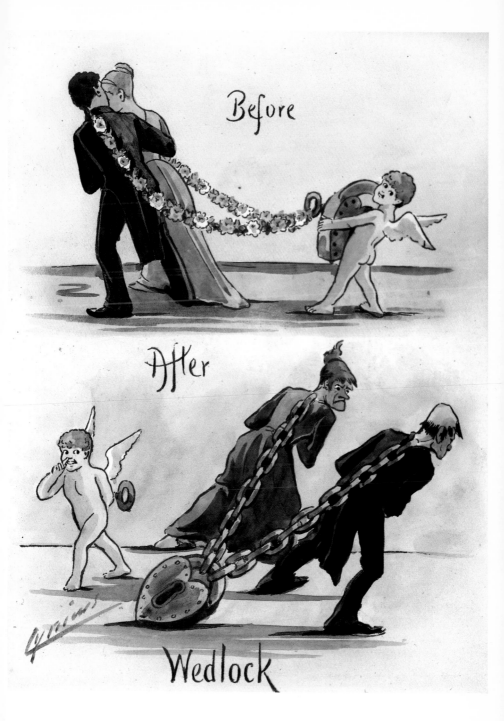

His latest purchase

Both Rich & Poor alike
Their nakedness display
The Poor because they <u>must</u>
The Rich because they <u>May</u>_

The Poor man makes it ;
The Rich man takes it.

THE FATAL SMILE

A Fairy Tale

Written and Illustrated

by

CYNICUS

THE ILLUSTRATIONS COLOURED BY HAND

Published at his STUDIO,
59 DRURY LANE, STRAND, LONDON.
1892.

Break, Break, Break!
"I would that my soul could utter
the thoughts that arise in me."
Tennyson

Going to a Funeral

Returning from a Funeral

8914-5   Scottish Character Sketches, from the Originals by Cynicus

If you "paint yourself,"
come to HASTINGS

"Away! ye gay landscapes"
Byron

10369

Our Excursion to Aberfeldy

Wishing you many a pleasant Cup of Tea

The Post Office had unwittingly done itself a good turn, though the extra burden made postmen agitate for higher wages. Yorkshire and Glasgow for once rivalled London in output. By 1904 Miller & Lang in Glasgow were producing a million cards a week.

Cynicus's old vignette designs were not wasted. The blank portion on the front of the card was now inscribed in Cynicus's own hand with a letter full of puns. The golfer writes ebulliently: 'It strikes me very forcibly golf is a much more exciting pastime than is generally supposed. What with long drives, balls and high tees, our time is fully occupied. I notice various people have been struck with my new club,' etc. The cyclist writes: 'I can confidently recommend it to anyone who feels run down or upset. By the way, I ran across an old friend the other day....We now share rooms at the Cottage Hospital....Yours enTyrely.'

After the Post Office's rule had been relaxed, the pictures took up the whole width or length of the card. Out came the pile of old *Quiz* back-numbers once more. Out came the old motifs of umbrellas and raging picnic weather, including his 1891 *Pall Mall Budget* sketches. In due course the working class could enjoy for a penny a sketch that their betters had paid guineas for in bound form, for of course the albums

Scots wha hae & Scots wha hinna'

were quarried for subjects. There were the old formulae of thwarted romance, purgatorial marriage and hellish parenthood. But new themes kept coming. Cynicus, diverted from his preoccupation with politics, effervesced with fun.

And there was another vein to exploit. In addition to the set of Burns quotations, Cynicus transmogrified the small-town Scots around him, disguised them in the regulation kilts and Balmoral bonnets of nineteenth-century fantasy, provided them with whisky bottles and Burns and gamps and the Bible, and caught their ignoble attitudes. Among his works in progress in 1892 he had listed *Scotch Pictures,* probably the prototypes of this series. Since then, MacLaren's *Bonnie Brier Bush* and Crockett's *Stickit Minister* had made a fashion for Scotch humour and sentiment. Yet it was not till 1908 that he published 'Scottish Character Sketches', a group of three cards that each bore two drawings, 'from the Originals by Cynicus'. They were certainly drawn in 1892 and exhibited in Dundee in 1894. 'A Scottish Sabbath' shows, firstly, the family going to church, stiff with rectitude and their Sunday best; secondly, returning dishevelled in the teeth of a rainstorm. Another card shows the funeral-goer having his wing collar tweaked straight by his loving wife; on his return in a state of happy inebriety she meets him at the door with threatening broom. In the third, 'March Comes in like a Lion' without wiping his feet; the same wee wifie sends him out like a lamb.

Was Cynicus consciously a Scot or consciously anti-Scottish? Up till his return to Tayport he did not seem to have thought much about it. His literary education had taken in the English poets with but a token Scot and Irishman or two. Barrie and Stevenson referred to themselves in print as Englishmen, and Scotland had been replaced on the map by North Britain. Surrounded now by Scottish Lowlanders of the traditional sort he could hardly have helped satirising them.

The most famous and beloved representation of the *perfervidum ingenium Scotorum* is the postcard entitled 'Wha Daur Meddle Wi' Me'. We see a tiny furious scarlet-faced creature, first cousin to Eliza the manic laundrymaid, its Balmoral bonnet rammed down, in its hand a pennant bearing the national motto. On a closer look we discover that the imp is not human at all but vegetable. It is the Scotch thistle.

The card was overprinted at one stage with a riddle and decorated the menu at a banquet given for the future Edward VII. At another time it was used by an Edinburgh shop to advertise, of all things, 'dainty lace handkerchiefs'. It was re-issued by Valentine & Sons and by others. The fact that this unflattering symbol of their character was taken to their hearts explains something about the Scots and warns us not to deduce from his caricatures that Cynicus was anti-Scot.

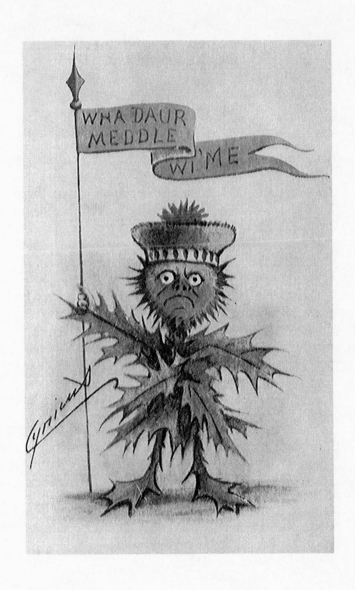

The Laird of Castle Cynicus

Castle Cynicus

As soon as the Company took over The Grove in 1902 Cynicus moved out. Just as once he had abandoned the workplace in Drury Lane for a villa in Barnes he now abandoned Tayport for Balmullo, at that time no more than a row of cottages sited above Leuchars on the slopes of Lucklaw Hill. Such was his confidence, he had not waited to see how the Company would fare before embarking on his grand scheme. He would have a country seat, the traditional reward of Victorian prosperity.

For £74 down and a bond for £426, and the obligations of feuduty, cess, schoolmaster's salary, minister's stipend, bishop's rents and victual payable to the governor of Edinburgh Castle—ancient burdens, partly in abeyance—he bought thirteen acres on the sunny slope above the hamlet.

Since the land already afforded a place of sorts to stay, a small cottage, Martin moved in at Whitsun; forty-eight years old and on his own for the first time.

He had been to Dundee to find an architect who would carry out his individualistic design; he had agreed with the proprietor of Lucklaw quarry to take stone for building; and now he stayed in the cottage to oversee every detail as his dream took shape. It was to be his answer to all those in London who thought he was finished. It would have a tall tower to look down on the panorama of his childhood haunts—his birthplace Leuchars; Guardbridge and the Eden estuary; Tentsmuir; the sweep of golden sand and golf links stretching to St Andrews.

In the course of confessing how as a youngster he had lured the rheumatic Miss Anderson into the sea Cynicus was impelled to mention that her brother built Battlefield House, Langside, 'with the Scottish Regalia sculptured at the corner, to commemorate the famous battle'. The contrast with their first cramped and crowded quarters in an artisan area of Cambuslang had so imprinted this picture on his memory that when eventually he built his own house he had his own insignia carved over the entrance—Truth the Lyre. If only his parents could have seen it!

Eager for publicity, he met the *People's Journal* reporter at Leuchars Junction one December day in 1902. The paper gave him two columns and three illustrations and described how he 'led the way to Balmullo, tramping cheerily through the "glaur" [mud]... pulling off his "Tammie" and swinging it merrily in one hand, then "rugging" it on his locks as if bearing it an illwill, and all the time talking in a most interesting manner of his experiences in London, speaking of the literary notabilities and artists whom he knows intimately, the conversation flying here, there and everywhere.'

By Christmas the builders were putting the roof on the main wing. What arose on Lucklaw was unique. Inside, the main feature was a forty-foot long studio. On one side stood the forty-five-foot tower, three storeys high, with windows facing in all directions. On the other side stretched a long glazed gallery like a conservatory. Studio and gallery were reared on a lower storey consisting of a south-facing sitting room, kitchen and 'offices', workshop and engine house. Bedrooms would be in the tower, one room per storey, with a museum at the top. An iron staircase led up from the museum to the flat roof, which offered extensive views.

Really it was just a seven-roomed house, a bachelor residence; but the rugged walls of red Balmullo felsite, the arched doorway and lintels of red Lochmaben sandstone, the massive grey Caithness slates, the tower, and above all the imposing site, so impressed the locals it was soon dubbed 'Cynicus Castle'. The owner was enchanted. Again, as with the caravan, there is a hint of Toad Hall.

Building the house did not distract him from his duty. Rather did his energy increase as the walls rose. While the rest of the family remained in Tayport he cycled daily to work from the 'castle'. He promptly bonded it for £1,350, and continued during the life of the Company to use it as security for borrowing useful sums.

The money thus obtained went towards furnishing the 'castle'. While still staying in the cottage he had begun assembling a fantastic collection of furnishings: a harp, a piano, cases of beetles and butterflies, antique swords and daggers—a boy's dream. So the visitor was greeted in the entrance hall by stuffed animals. He found the large studio sumptuously decorated with rich dark wall coverings, an ornate frieze, and a ceiling beamed and stuccoed. He was led to admire two large Cynicus paintings of sunrise and sunset at the inner end of the long room. Between them was a small pipe organ (or perhaps the harmonium in disguise), and elsewhere in the room stood the harp and the baby grand piano. His attention would be drawn to six painted wall panels illustrating Shakespearean characters; his host was rightly proud of those and reproduced them as postcards.

Red plush easy chairs on a polar bear rug made a more intimate setting at a fireplace; and on the mantelpiece an ornate French clock and side ornaments completed the tribute to Victorian taste. In a glass case in the anteroom sat a mummy said to be an Inca princess.

He was proud of the museum he had made in the tower, where he was still adding to his collection of curios. There were stuffed birds and animals, those cases of butterflies and beetles and birds' eggs, African masks, a purple coat that had reputedly belonged to Prince Charlie, box upon box of gems, semi-precious stones, flints and Roman coins. There was a slab of bending sandstone, a Saracen's helmet, Greek pottery, old armour, a skull taken a from a plague pit in the Strand, and more and more. Some of the exhibits were bought because they were beautiful, some because they were romantic, and some because he was conned by dealers. Friends supplied more from exotic locations. Among local people and the visitors who were conducted round the collection it was presumed that Cynicus had gathered the exhibits during his travels abroad in the caravan—quite apocryphal travels, of course. He said himself that a waitress's weekly tips would have paid for all the travelling abroad he had ever done. Fortunately he never knew what became of the collection.

The grounds were also lovingly set out with fruit trees, shrubs, and flowers; stone was brought to lay paths and create a terrace and steps; and a sundial and garden seats were placed to advantage.

The money began to run out before the house was quite finished. Though an engine house had been built, he did not consider an electricity generator a priority, so oil lamps remained the only form of lighting; similarly, though the house was plumbed he put off connecting the piping to a water supply, since there was a handy well, and that

Castle Cynicus

continued to be the water source. A balcony was intended to run right round the front of the house at first-floor level, on to which the french windows were intended to open; that balcony too was postponed for ever and french windows opened on to space.

When visitors came, as they often did—for Cynicus found it impossible to live without company—it was a problem where to put them. The cottage

"THE LIGHT OF OTHER DAYS."

was pressed into service, or beds were put up in the library and conservatory.

Cynicus so enjoyed his fine new house he threw it open to the public at every opportunity. Any casual passerby was welcome to enter and examine the museum. He installed billiards, bagatelle and carpet bowls to amuse guests, and bought three dozen handchairs for the audience at lectures and concerts, and for sitting out at dances.

In March 1905, for instance, he would stage a Grand Concert in aid of the Road Improvement Fund, an evening of songs, recitations and dance, admission one shilling. The house and avenue were to be illuminated, not with electricity in the continuing absence of a generator, but with Chinese lanterns.

Cynicus unassumingly headed his writing paper 'Balmullo' and half jokingly called the house 'Liberty Hall'; but the locals called it 'Cynicus Castle', and that name stuck, appearing later as the official name on Ordnance Survey maps. Cynicus much preferred the ring of 'Castle Cynicus'.

All this would have meant little, however, without Bob.

'My Days Of Adversity Are At An End'

In January 1903 a railway signalman in Leuchars called his latest offspring Martin Anderson Graham. Bob Graham was three years younger than Cynicus. Possibly they had been friends from childhood. (Was Bob the 'friend in the railway service' who wangled the young artist a free ticket to Carlisle on his first trip south? Was he even the reason Martin adopted the pseudonym of 'Bob' in *Quiz*?) Physically they were opposites, the railwayman broad and phlegmatic, the slender artist like a coiled spring. As he often accused Bob of having all a Scotsman's reticence about expressing his feelings, being made a godfather was a gratifying display of affection. Theirs was a boyish friendship of constant visits and shared jokes. It was also a very Victorian friendship in the sentimental expressions of undying affection; both were given to penning mawkish verse.

Bob kept the greeting that Cynicus sent him for his forty-sixth birthday.

> My dear chum Bob,
>
> Another stage of Life's fair journey is reached today and finds us nearer dearer still. As we pass on by sunny paths and flowery meadows through darkening woods where shadows fall, then out again into the radiant sunshine of Life's afternoon may we, still hand in hand with those we love about us pass on into the glorious realms that lie beyond.
>
> The Birthday wish of your affectionate Chum,
> Martin.

Under the soulful wording of the birthday letter we seem to see references to the writer's sunny childhood, the shadows of his last years in London, and the assurance that life henceforward would be sweet. When in 1904 Bob and family moved from Leuchars to take up another post in Burntisland, Cynicus wrote an emotional 'Farewell' and added a codicil to his will to ensure that on his death Bob would receive a pound a week for life passing to his widow.

This private sentimentality contrasts with the pungency of the satires. His professional persona and his social self were greatly at odds, the cartoonist bitter and angry, the friend and host kindly, lovable and considerate. It is tempting to view the cartoons as a safety valve for suppressed feelings. His sunny nature automatically swept unpleasant topics out of sight. He was a master at concealing negative emotion, perhaps too eager for admiration to burden others with his disappointments, too proud to admit to anything but success, or too defensive to let the outside world see behind the mask. Yet very, very occasionally anger slipped its leash, and was all the worse for having been pent up. Cynicus suppressed all reference to the London rupture for years, and for years it rankled. In December 1904 it erupted again.

Whether Keary's loan of a hundred pounds was made out to William or Martin or the London publishing company, Cynicus refused to repay it. Either by letter or in a face to face interview he and William had another violent quarrel. On William the poisonous claws inflicted festering wounds. Apparently Cynicus made his refusal a matter of principle. Keary compromised. In place of a money repayment with interest he would take pictures. But he must have them by the last day of the year. Cynicus sent him a letter of dignified reproof—and kept a copy.

Dear Mr Keary,

As required I have finished the pictures to the "Time limit." I feel you will not be pleased and I am greatly vexed to have to complete them so hastily. Fortunately, as "it is not so nominated in the bond" I am not obliged to sign them. You have made it too much a matter of usury and percentages to command my best work. Your advance (£100) was made to my brother during my absence in Scotland and was offered not asked, my only participation in it being to sign the bond which you have held over me with interest for ten years making the amount about £150. During that time I have had to struggle with misfortune and adversity, and when it was in your power to help me by giving my work a place in your magazines I appealed in vain, my approved contributions were withheld and are in your possession now, presumably as security for your advance. My last request for recognition in your publications was in 1900 and was unanswered. Fortunately my days of adversity are at an end and with the pictures goes the last of your claim upon me, nevertheless I have to thank you that when in your power you did not press me as hard as you might have done. For my own credit—as well as yours—I am willing, if you are, to put as much additional work in these pictures as will make them at least worthy of my signature.

With good wishes and kind remembrances,

Yours sincerely,

Cynicus.

About 1906 the Grahams moved to Balmullo and Cynicus was able to spend his free time with his bosom friend. These were happy days, 'in the radiant sunshine of life's afternoon'.

While Bob was on Sunday duty in his signalbox Cynicus wrote him a note 'to relieve the monotony of your habitual Sabbath desecration' and tell him that his fourteen-year-old son Davie was at the castle for an art lesson.

As I opened my iron box just now my eye caught the date on my will 14th Nov 05—"Dear! Dear! now more than a year." Undoubtedly the most important event since that time is your coming to Balmullo. I cannot help feeling and I think you feel too it has been better for the welfare of your family and certainly it has been better for our friendship. Of course you are so confoundedly reticent it would be the last thing in the world for you to say so but I have learnt to read your thoughts by your actions and looks which are far more eloquent than your tongue. For instance it would never do for you to say you were pleased to see me but I know you would be jolly mad if I didn't come and I should just be as vexed if you didn't want me, so Providence has adjusted matters by making two wayward natures totally dependent on each other for much of their happiness, the result being one of the sweetest friendships of Modern times.

The point of the letter was to remind Bob of the codicil in his favour. Was the depth of feeling just a little one-sided that he felt moved to mention his will as an inducement? Bob was obviously fond of him and, of course, flattered to have such a famous friend.

Wherever he looked, Cynicus could be pleased with himself. Everything was once more as rosy as it had been back in London in the early 1890s. Although no longer hailed as an advanced social critic, he had the satisfaction of being a highly popular and still satirical postcard artist. Perhaps he was truer to his socialist instincts when printing penny postcards for the masses than when producing hand-coloured guinea books for the social élite.

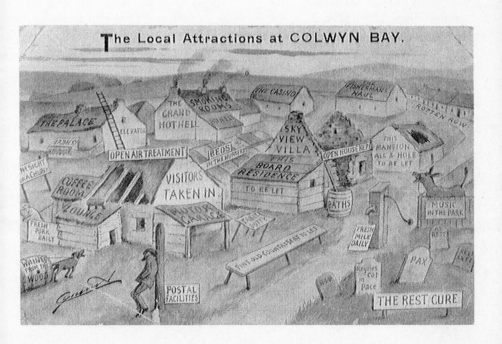

Chapter 12—The Postcard Craze 1904–07

THE POSTCARD CRAZE was under way. Postcards and postage were so cheap that every class of society could take it up. What had begun as a middle-class hobby now realised vast sales to the working class. In one year alone (1904) they sent four hundred and twenty million picture postcards. Not just on holiday, at any time, people fired off bundles of cards to their friends in the hope of receiving bundles back. They would send a whole set at once to the same person. Cynicus took advantage of this mania to spread a limerick over four cards, which would be sent off one per postal collection to puzzle and amuse the recipient. It is unlikely that all the purchasers saw the fun of misapplied literary quotations, but they loved the drawings, and wrote cheeky remarks on them.

We who are spoiled for colour and design, from cornflakes packets to television advertisements, find it hard to appreciate the hunger for visual stimulation felt by the working class of those days. Newspapers and magazines were miserly of illustration; what there was was black and white. Clothes were black or grey; at any one time much of the population would be wearing mourning. Underwear was white, shirts were white, sheets were white, cheap crockery was white. Interiors were painted to resemble dark wood. House plants were dark green non-flowering aspidistras and castor-oil plants. Small wonder that the colourful postcard collection was treasured and added to at every opportunity. Tayport shared in the boom.

Cynicus started to design more postcards specifically with postcard buyers in mind. He mined the theme of holidays for the masses, with memories of Glaswegians 'doon the watter'. He crowded the beach with warmly dressed figures, crowded them into the sea in decorous striped bathing drawers. His old folk went on mass picnics, but instead of consuming tea and gossiping, as befitted their age, they danced a joyous eightsome reel and sported at seesaw and leapfrog. (Such a theme came in useful years later when Lloyd George brought in the old age pension.) The young in heart were his subject; at this stage the young in years were conspicuously absent. Each decade has its favoured age; for the Edwardians it was middle age.

Even as he worked on new motifs, he sifted his store of past productions for postcard material, whether cartoon or landscape. Yes, the landscapes were now being bought as postcards.

As usual, the work of Cynicus drew mixed reactions. There was no problem with the buying public; the cards were selling almost faster than the company could produce them. But the arbiters of taste, as represented by postcard magazines, found fault with his sense of humour. The *Picture Postcard and Collectors' Chronicle* found seasickness 'a very unpleasant subject unfit for portrayal on a postcard'. Later it hedged: 'It appears to us that one either dislikes his work or else thinks it is some of the cleverest and most wonderful in the world.'

The new company was full of innovation and commercial verve. It was not long before the same cards were being reissued with the names of particular holiday resorts added. For example, the original design 'On the Sands' would then reappear with a placename as 'On the Sands at Lundin Links', and so forth. The Cynicus Publishing Company Ltd is thought to be the originator of this new sales ploy. It was so successful it became standard practice with other publishers.

Responsible for the commercialism was most probably John Allan, now Managing Director. He toured to publicise Cynicus and his work with lantern lectures. The company advertised the postcards in national publications and the golf prints in a local paper.

"CYNICUS."
(By himself.)

In its first two years the Company had made profits of £1,400 and £1,500, and paid an 8% dividend. In 1904 the assets were reckoned at £15,560 and the liabilities at £3,072. So at least said the Company's prospectus for an issue of 4,000 6% cumulative preference shares to provide additional working capital. Simon G Fraser JP of Dundee had joined the board of directors. Mrs Anne Campbell, the Perth aunt, bought some shares. Employees of the firm showed their confidence in it by taking holdings, including one of the artists, C G L Phillips. Shareholders were spread over the Scottish Lowlands in clumps as if the good news of a prime investment was passed on by word of mouth.

At that time company law did not require the annual publication of accounts. The accounts of the Cynicus Publishing Company Ltd were presumed to be in order.

Nineteen hundred and four was a leap year, and the first leap year for some time, since 1900 was not. The Company made the most of it, proclaiming theirs to be the 'first and only cards designed for Leap Year'. Two sweet, romantic designs were a hit. 'An Old-stile Courtship' portrayed a couple kissing on a stile, framed by her red parasol. 'You and I By and Bye' were a rotund, contented old pair. *Quiz* and the *Humours of Cynicus* once more offered satirical comments on romance and courtship. The nubile fat lady asked us again to 'Consider My Sighs'; the unprepossessing one with a bag of money said, 'Now's Your Chance'; a young man, 'Declining Age', fended off an eager oldster; while a girl, such is sex discrimination, threw herself at an old man, crying, 'Say Yes!'; and the wiry female in her mutch and slippers took off on a broomstick for the man in the moon, as 'Her Last Resource'. (These would always come in handy for Valentines as well.)

Runaway Success

The Company went from strength to strength. Although it still produced a number of hand-painted cards it could offer the trade its staff of colourists for hand-colouring collotype, half-tone and black and white postcards, for jewelling and tinselling. To reduce the reliance on Cynicus's own output and tickle the fancy of other tastes it advertised photographic prints of popular actresses and local views. It also brought out novelty cards, such as the 'Bachelor's Button' with a real button on it, and others with a real shamrock, an oak leaf, heather, moss, a scrap of oatcake, either glued on or under transparent paper, a piece of linoleum ('This Will Floor You') and so on. For the quality trade well-known artists were employed and allowed to do what they were best at. James Douglas RSW did a set of local watercolour sketches. Wilkie Kilgour provided 'London by Moonlight', the Lake District and a set of the Clyde, very different from Cynicus's 'doon the watter'. From the versatile 'Jotter' came views of Cornwall and the Lake District, and a good draughtsman like C G L Phillips could turn out acceptable cityscapes. 'Soon our staff numbered over a hundred, and we had won the highest award for colour printing in the country.'

'Our Local Express' was pulled along by a valiant donkey and pushed by passengers and dozy railwaymen, while another part of the numerous crew enjoyed a game of cricket, the tea kettle boiled on the engine, and a woman on the line held up a notice commanding—Not So Fast. 'Our Local Express' was issued with the train crew playing golf or cricket. By 1907 Cynicus was able to report that millions of this design had been sold.

Some of the holiday series became deservedly popular. 'We Two', the tubby couple whose back view we observe as they gaze contentedly out to sea, continued for years with varying captions. 'Mixed Bathing' perhaps shows us what they were seeing—a crowd making acquaintance with the briny. The holidaymakers found lodgings in 'Our Village', where the pace of life was equally slow, at the inn called The Golden Fleas, and drank 'milk' straight from the village pump. The middle class took their guns to a Fife-style farm for 'Our Shooting Party' and inflicted heavy casualties on the denizens of the farmyard.

For persons with a tarter taste, there were prints and cartoons: 'His Latest Purchase' is a young girl paired off with the archetypal capitalist; originally from the Labor Leader 'Both Rich and Poor' display their flesh,

parliament pro-rogued

the one as *décolletage,* the other through holes in her rags; 'Young England' is represented by three louts playing cards, with alcohol and tobacco at hand; 'Ladies of the Court' is the definitive version of three female pugilists; and 'The Wolf and the Lamb' are the sour-faced matron with her henpecked husband.

Nineteen six brought a General Election. Cynicus could not resist issuing his favourite political cartoons, including from *Cartoons Social and Political* 'Land for the People' and 'The New Jerusalem', from the 1895 election his attacks on self-serving politicians 'Going to Parliament' and 'Parliament Pro-rogued', and the voter as an overburdened donkey tempted by the candidate's carrots in 'Wooing the Donkey'.

Quiz provided more fun: 'Hark the Lark' declaims the family looking up to spot it; while a charging cow again tosses 'Away ye Gay Landscapes!' Another series of *Quiz* black humour contains the robbing of birds' nests, an aggressive goat, two suicides, and the boy falling on to railings ('Something to Fall Back Upon').

The woman from *Quiz* in mutch and shawl has gone modern: she has taken to riding a bicycle and playing cricket. In Cynicus's cartoons the women are usually larger than the men and frequently tower over them, as they towered over him—surely a gift to Freudians. He never made jokes about short people like himself; in fact, there are a few complimentary postcards on that topic.

The *Picture Postcard and Collectors' Chronicle* still objected to Cynicus's 'rather jaundiced view of life' and disapproved of any cards in which 'the jarring note of cynicism is struck'. It much preferred the sets of hand-tinted actresses and photographs of sugary children. But by now Cynicus knew to stick to the formulae that had made his a household name. Experimentation had been knocked out of him. Indeed, his humour was now remarkably little changed from the 1880s, as though he were psychologically arrested in the era when five siblings and Mother lived together in Broughty Ferry and each week thought up new comic sketches for *Quiz*.

The following year the postcard magazine took the Company to task for the low standard of hand-painting on Cynicus cards. Possibly the Company attracted more outside custom than it could cope with and had to employ more youngsters than Annie could ever hope to train and supervise.

In 1906 Cynicus signed himself General Manager, but it is clear that he was not fully his own boss. Allan, who kept a close eye on what lines sold and what remained on the stationers' shelves, demanded less satire and fewer literary allusions, more holiday scenes and lots more young romance. The postcard buying public wanted nothing highbrow, just simple fun. Cynicus found himself producing courtship at a dance, in the park, on a swing, in a rocking chair, in a wildly rocking boat, with and without a chaperon. Lines of identical young couples overpopulate 'The Lovers Walk' (1907), a design so popular that it was pirated by Tacon & Co. Cynicus took them to law and won.

He preferred the holiday experience, the luggage-laden hunt for lodgings, the overcrowded accommodation, the overloaded tram or boat or train that took holiday-makers there and back, the fun of seaside frolics. Seething crowds were a favourite feature of the holiday designs—'Our Picnic to…', 'The Last Car to…' and 'The Last Car from…' on which he crammed nearly two hundred passengers.

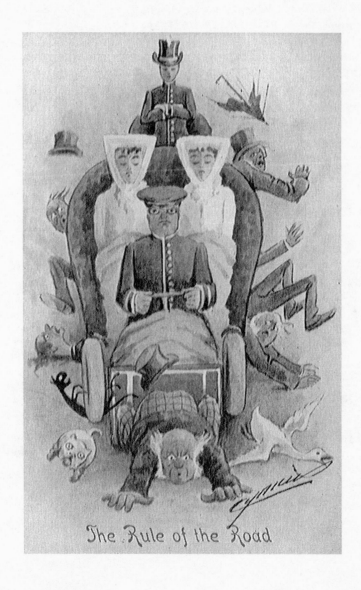

The Rule of the Road

Motoring was a dangerous pursuit. The Cynicus motoring set is priceless, both for the transfer to the motorcar of horse carriage habits, such as a lackey on the dickey-seat, and for Cynicus's hazy conception of a motorcar. It is not only a horseless but an engineless carriage, a sort of three-piece suite on wheels. One party displays the smug superiority of 'The Rule of the Road', as their chauffeur imperturbably mows down pedestrians and animals; while another less experienced party sits petrified with horror. The end of the outing is inevitable: return on foot in bandages, while the donkey from 'Our Local Express' pulls the contraption home.

In 1907 Marion and Lizzie decided to venture 100 shares each in the Company. The North of Scotland Bank took a thousand ordinary shares. Nobody saw anything ominous in this, of course, but it was. The Bank already held the title deeds of the family's properties and of the Company's headquarters.

**If you're downhearted
Come to Arundel**

Chapter 13—Boom and Bust 1907–11

TO THE PUBLIC, Cynicus was little changed from his Drury Lane days, still full of wit and fun. With his gift of the common touch, he had people on his side. When he walked into the commercial room of a hotel, the barman was pleased to see him give as good as he got. His *en brosse* hairstyle had attracted the attention of a would-be wit.

'Hullo! What's making your hair stand on end?'

'Amazement at your impertinence,' was the ready response.

On another occasion, while walking near the harbour of Tayport, he noticed some turnips floating in with the tide. Turning to an old fisherman he asked if that was why they called it a 'neep' tide. [Scots neep=turnip] A look of bewilderment crept across the fisherman's features as he exclaimed, 'Eh, Mr Anderson, but I thocht a man o' your education wad ken better than that!'

He called his dog Askit, and when anyone asked him its name replied: 'Ask it.'

He was always happy to go anywhere and deliver comic lectures. For such topics as 'Fife in Olden Times' or 'The Humours of Scotland' he used his stock of magic lantern slides and appropriate exhibits from the museum, such as old weaponry.

He loved to stroll on Lucklaw Hill behind his house, enjoying the panorama of land and sea by day and stargazing by night. Villagers who met him there presumed he was in league with poachers. Perhaps he was.

Being on familiar terms with half the neighbourhood and Dundee he was never short of guests. Besides, he had his special friend Bob. Since Cynicus was always willing to tutor young talent, Bob's son David walked up to the castle many an evening and learned to imitate the master's style. In return he acted as errand boy, and his father looked after the castle's pony and trap.

When Cynicus felt the urge to rove he still had the caravan. Business transport, however, was the bicycle. In velvet jacket (dressing the part of artist) with knickerbockers and tam o'shanter (dressing the part of laird) he cycled every morning the five miles from Balmullo to Tayport; every evening he pedalled back up the steep hill to the castle. He attached a reading frame to the handlebars and read a book on smoother stretches. Though now in his early fifties Cynicus had the

Here will I pledge thee,
dearest one

figure of a youth, and kept it till the end. He rationed his food even before poverty forced rationing on him.

At the end of 1907 he was interviewed by a Dundee paper, the *Weekly Welcome*. He was the same entertaining host he had been in Drury Lane, and this journalist, like earlier interviewers in London, succumbed to the charm: 'An evening spent here with the laird of Cynicus Castle is an evening that one will always look back upon with considerable pleasure.'

Cynicus gave him his philosophy of art, his personal secret of success. It had not changed in the fifteen years since it appeared in the *Humours*, and it would not change in the succeeding twenty-five:

Brevity is the soul of wit, and to be successful as a cartoonist it is necessary to be to the point. Put nothing into your sketch that is not absolutely necessary and what you do put in see that it is humorous and in keeping. It is in this that so many cartoonists fail. They crowd their sketches with side issues that detract attention from the point of the picture.

His method of working was to have no method. 'For days I will never touch a brush, but when I strike an idea it does not take me long to work it off.'

> I don't regard my postcards with any great satisfaction. I am sorry that the public will not have what I think better. I have been blamed for being vulgar, but where broad humour is concerned it is difficult to say what is vulgar and what is not. The people I am catering for with the penny card do not want high art, and I have to begin with the thing they will have in the hope that they may be led on to better as we go along.
>
> There is a never-ending demand for love scenes. It does not matter how ridiculous it is, if it is a love scene the public will have it. Anything with a local application is also sure to be successful, and therefore I try to hit the whole world.

If he thought he could educate the taste of the buying public through this accessible medium he was deluding himself. The masses wanted fun and sentiment, a little social comment but no political ideas. What is more, it is said wholesale agents and shopkeepers boycotted his political cards. Far from gradually increasing, social criticism was rapidly disappearing and in 1908 Cynicus was drawing—for the first time—new postcards showing romantic couples with little or no satirical edge to the picture, simply kissing and cuddling.

In 1908 Sir James Caw brought out *Scottish Painting Past and Present 1620-1908*. Although Cynicus was deemed worthy of inclusion, the author had not a good word to say about him: 'The satire of "Cynicus" is more broad than subtle, and his comedy is apt to degenerate into somewhat vulgar farce, while his artistry is facile without strength or quality.' By this time Cynicus was well accustomed to, if not hardened against the steady denigration of his art. He could console himself with the knowledge that years of booming postcard sales proved the general public was of another opinion.

More and more designs had to be pumped out quickly, for 1908 was a boom year. At the peak of production some substandard designs were published. John Allan, the firm's manager, had a facility for saccharine ideas. He wrote feeble jingles and Bob Graham's son David, as a trainee artist, paired them with more or less apposite vignettes to produce trashy greetings card stuff. Sentimental verses and flowers ran easily off the production line. Stationers took them with the rest of the stock, and they sold as well if not better.

Economy of effort meant overprinting with topical or local references. Other firms issued special cards to exploit the Scottish National Exhibition of 1908; the Tayport company simply overprinted romantic cards that were already in stock. To mark the inauguration of the

"Strangers yet"

Boy Scout movement Cynicus just wittily changed the caption of a card where girl pursues man to 'Scouting for Boys'. And considering the immense number of oldsters and crabbed-age-and-youth couples in his opus, he made surprisingly little of Lloyd George's 1909 Old Age Pension Act. It was partly that his interest had waned. He had tired of churning out popular designs.

In 1909 a sixpenny paperback *Selections from Cynicus* was published. It was a pleasant book with many light-hearted cartoons taken from the *Satires*, the *Humours, Symbols and Metaphors,* and none from *Cartoons Social and Political.* It was a modest success.

Later in the year came the North Pole controversy. Peary got there. Did Cook? The company reissued any card with the slightest chance of making a North Pole allusion—'Sealed With Love' (two nuzzling seals) was inaptly overprinted 'Cook and Peary at the North Pole'; and the apoplectic thistle 'Wha Daur Meddle Wi' Me' naturally claimed to have been at the Pole himself.

The Craze Passes

The pace was hectic. Thousand upon thousand of the distinctive cards crisscrossed Britain and the colonies. CPC Ltd was one of the big employers in Tayport and there seemed to be no reason why it should not continue to expand; but the end was coming quickly. As with so many crazes of the early twentieth century—ping-pong, diabolo, roller-skating—the novelty was wearing off. Postcard collecting was not in the same class as cycling, say, where weekend pleasure was combined with weekday utility. It was strictly a luxury. As a stage in the twentieth century progression from colour print to colour television the postcard was being superseded by moving pictures. In the 1908-09 depression working people could not support two luxuries. A weekly visit to the cinema would mop up all their spare cash.

In 1908 two directors and the company secretary resigned. The new secretary was James Alcock, the local agent of the Company's bank, the North of Scotland. Mr Alcock's allegiance was bound to be divided. The issued capital now stood at 2,028 preference shares and 10,650 ordinary shares, belonging to 36 shareholders.

The first signs of dwindling profitability came in the next balance-sheet, with debts of £3,456 balanced by goodwill of £3,768. There were hints in Tayport that some director was filling his own pocket at the expense of the trusting Cynicus. Cynicus himself was to heap the blame on the North of Scotland Bank. A look at the business done in the Company's shares is revealing. Apart from the bank—which was still hanging on for its own ends, Cynicus was to say—and Allan, who still had enough faith in the firm to retain a large holding, the

[Courtesy of N.E. Fife District Museum Service]

bigger and possibly more knowledgable shareholders were getting out. Only mug money was coming in. Among the mugs, sisters Marion and Lizzie Anderson added to their holdings. The big new money—£1,600 of ordinary shares—came from the Baptist Union in Glasgow and Edinburgh. Comic postcards were expected to finance its home and foreign missions.

It is usual to assume that Cynicus was easily cheated, an unworldly artist with no business sense. But postcard manufacturers with plenty of business sense were failing likewise, Blum & Degen for one. The tide had turned. It was sweeping their profits away as swiftly as it had swept them in. The Company's plant, valued at £1,687, was only valuable when in production. The stock of cards which made up so much of their assets (£6,585) was only valuable as long as it was being taken up by stationers. The blocks and copyrights, entered at the conservative valuation of £1,962, were valueless if not turned into cards that sold. Goodwill would vanish like a puff of smoke if—unthinkably—the Company were wound up.

By the next year the profit and loss account was showing a deficit of £895. The traveller from London still called, David Graham still turned out adaptations of Cynicus's own designs, Cynicus still went out sketching in his caravan, and the blockmakers still received orders for new blocks. Young Graham remarked in his diary that business was very slow but put it down to the King's death. Cynicus tried to scrape a little cash together by selling his garden produce. He printed a postcard to advertise his 'Balmullo Strawberries'. Dundee shops took flowers and fruit but did not pay for them. There was no money about. The mines and railways were on strike.

When Cynicus paid off his £1,350 bond on the castle, he had taken out a new bond for £750 with the North of Scotland Bank. This bank now controlled his own and the family's property and all the Company's property as well.

In November 1910 David Graham noted in his diary that the auditor had arrived. The following day the news was out: the Company's finances were more than shaky. Already the Bank was 'pressing'.

Cynicus was galvanised into action. Next day he despatched David to Dundee library for books and every day or two thereafter for information. Cynicus was going to save the firm by writing a book. By the 20th of January 1911 it was finished; by the 25th David was told it was sold out and was sent up to the castle to see about a second edition. It was not sold out; it had merely been distributed to the trade.

Cynicus fought to retain his business in the only way he knew, which was to catch public attention. Although postcard sales were collapsing, he might still be able to sell a book if he brought out something daring. The new work was an unusual booklet entitled *Who shall rule: Briton or*

Norman? To his own satisfaction it settled an old score with those Southerners who had failed to appreciate *Cartoons Social and Political* and so hastened his departure from London. The South of England was an effete, static society with people frozen in feudal positions; the North was the place for enterprise, intelligence and vitality.

Would it sell?

O, for a man—
　　O, for a man—
　　O, for a mansion in the skies !

Chapter 14—Disasters 1911–14

IN FEBRUARY 1911 came financial collapse. Cynicus kept a diary during March and April, to which he confided the thoughts he hid from public view. The 'fatal smile' was as essential a part of him as it was of the hero of that fairy story. When at the end of his tether, rather than confide in another person he would write his fears down for the eyes of an understanding posterity. Just before the March AGM he wrote in the diary:

> 1st March 1911 The Bank has refused to help us any more as our business does not seem to be paying. I just managed to get the servants wages today but have nothing for my taxes and other accounts long past due... One awfully sad thing to me is that my new book 'Briton or Norman' doesn't seem to have caught on and I had put great hope in it, that it might have been a success and helped us all. Mr Allan is lecturing about me and my work in a hall in Dundee tonight. How little the people think who will be laughing and applauding my pictures and verses what my thoughts are. I am wondering if at my age, nearly 57, it can be possible for me to do some striking work in cartoons and pictures to help us all in our trouble.

With desperate determination to look on the bright side he added: 'The good news. Our artichokes were dug today and there were 5 big sacks full.'

The business he calculated to be a mere £500 in the red, with assets of £6,000 and liabilities of £6,500, but that was by valuing the stock of cards at £2,100 and a thousand originals at £500. This turned out to be a miscalculation.

When he reckoned up his private assets—Castle Cynicus; the Tayport house he had bought back from Aunt Campbell; his shares in the company, optimistically valued at half the issue price; and a legacy to come from another aunt in Surrey—the assets far outweighed his private overdraft of £770 plus the £750 bond over the castle. He disregarded recent loans from his sisters, 'which need not necessarily be repaid'.

Committed to paper the figures brought no relief.

> 2nd Mar. Passed a wretched night. Misery and foreboding. Got up about half past six feeling tired and exhausted. Bitter morning. Fortunately no letters. Got to Tayport, better news, £15 of orders in and business looks better than last year at same time. Mr Allan greatly pleased with his lecture. Hopeful there may be good word from London tomorrow [about his aunt's legacy].

Gathered sixteen Bunches Violets tonight, awfully pleased about it. O if my land could be made to keep me independent of the World... Busy now on Cartoons.

3rd Mar. Got up early and worked at garden. Had a depressing uneasy feeling—letter from grocer asking payment of a/c now £8.10/-. Word from London disappointing. It will be difficult to get money, possibly impossible... £14 of orders in, much ahead of last year. O if it would just continue... First Cartoon nearly finished.

Every Friday the gardener's boy took a cartload of flowers and vegetables to sell at market, but the return was trifling. 'Everything right but want of money,' Cynicus wrote.

At the weekend, Annie came out from Tayport and they walked over Lucklaw Hill making hopeful plans. He was able to appreciate the beauty of the sunrise. But on Monday—

Wet dismal morning. Worked hard in garden. Sad news from London—no hopes of raising £50... Strong desire to ask Mr Henderson for £25. Cannot screw up courage. God help us all. Finished 2nd Cartoon and begun 3rd... Have made up my mind to start painting pictures again.

Allan and he dreamed up unrealistic schemes for saving the business, such as a monthly magazine devoted to his works. This appealed to Cynicus and he started at once on sketches and songs, both words and music. He sent off the three cartoons to *Reynolds's Newspaper*, 'not very certain of success'. They were rejected.

That day Johnnie brought home fourteen shillings from the market, so it was possible to pay the handyman.

12th Mar. Went with Mr Henderson to Logie, had tea with the Laird, envied him his easy opulence, just before leaving with Mr Henderson summoned courage and asked him to help. He very generously offered at once. I asked the loan of £30 which he agreed to give. Tremendous relief. The shadows and clouds seemed at once to roll away. Met Bob immediately after. He seemed glad and relieved too.

Next day he paid the taxes, and rented out the caravan. It became a constant daily struggle to find the cash for bills and workers' wages. Orders for postcards were arriving, but no cash. Cynicus still cycled to Tayport every working day, then spent the evenings sketching. '27th... The Bank refused to honour further cheques unless cash in to meet them. Grave discussion Annie, Mr Allan, Hardie and I as to the wages this week.' He went to Dundee and borrowed £12 from his friend Norwell the painter. 'Very grateful.' Fortunately Norwell accepted four of James Douglas's watercolours in lieu of repayment. '29th... Great news at Tayport.' Voluntary liquidation was to be arranged. He was merry with relief that something was about to be resolved. 'Mr Allan suggests coming to stay here. I like the idea. It will be cheaper for us all. Banked £20 this week so wages seem secure.'

As if to show all was not lost, that day a sixpenny edition of the *Satires of Cynicus* was published, the first impression of 3,000 being taken up by the trade. Though the weather was bitterly cold Cynicus was driven to ever greater exertions in the garden. On the 30th the directors met to wind up the business. 'To me very pathetic though no one seemed to see it. It seemed another landmark in my life... Is it a turn downwards or upwards in my career? It's hard to say "All's for the best" but we must say it. It felt the same as being at a funeral.' Just a hint of characteristic optimism was trying to burst through, as he strained to believe it might be a 'turn upwards'.

Cynicus had spent all his capital on building and furnishing Castle Cynicus. Had it been a vain and foolish enterprise? The principal feature of the house, its great room built specifically for social gatherings, had

enriched his life and that of many others. Since Drury Lane days his way of life had been to provide the venue, to indulge his generosity, to offer constant hospitality and entertainments. 'I will try my best to save it,' he said, 'for this house has been built and everything has been done with the intention of leaving it as a public gift and a record of our family and of my work.' The paradox from *Symbols and Metaphors* was to be directly applicable:

The rock which wrecks the vessel,
May also save the crew.

Castle Cynicus, which had eaten up his financial reserves, would now be made to provide a meagre livelihood.

On the 11th of April Cynicus cycled to Tayport to woo the angry shareholders. With him in the chair they agreed on liquidation. Allan and Alcock were appointed liquidators. He cycled home carefree in the afternoon sunshine and got back to work in the garden.

On the 14th, his 57th birthday, he entered in his diary 'Not enough cash in for wages so have agreed (Mr Allan, Annie and I) not to take more than we absolutely require. Cart [with garden produce at market] not very successful 7/6.

'1st May. Mr Lawson has offered me his 2000 shares in our business for a throwaway consideration.' [They were worthless, of course.] At this last entry in the diary his natural optimism, forcibly constrained by events, breaks out: 'This, I think, will almost save the business which now practically belongs to our family. The tide of fortune seems to have turned at last.' With that happy illusion he was able to put the diary aside.

His optimism was misplaced. The bank wanted to liquidate the company's assets post haste. No thought was given to the best way of disposing of twelve hundred paintings and prints. Instead of being put out to art dealers in Edinburgh and London they were sent to a second-hand furniture saleroom in a neighbouring town and sold off 'without reserve'. In totting up his assets, Cynicus had estimated his originals at £500. They realised £50. The artist is said to have been present at the sale and to have bought some himself. He must have found it intolerably painful to witness the callous display of beloved items, the auctioneer's jokes, and the stinginess of the bidders. He lost nearly the whole of his life's work. Three hundred original paintings and drawings in oil and watercolour went for a penny each, seventy-four framed original water-colours for sevenpence each. An original that had realised over £4,000 in reproduction and another, of which nearly a million copies had been sold, brought four shillings apiece.

The unsold blocks were transported to the castle to join the unsold copies of *Cartoons Social and Political* and *Who Shall Rule: Briton or Norman?* Their fates varied. Some were hawked round Socialist meetings by Paddy Walsh. Some would be re-used down the remaining years of his life; some ended their existence in Leeds and some in Edinburgh; a few finally found homes when the castle was plundered.

Tayport had been alive with rumours of fraud. Certainly the figures in the 1910 and 1911 accounts—the first to be made public—do not quite add up. Perhaps the shares had been 'watered', with more being issued than could in due course sustain a dividend. Tayport pointed the finger at Allan, the most active of the directors and the Andersons' friend. For the next few years his every move was reported to Lizzie, and through Annie to Martin, who poohpoohed the idea. Allan had even proposed staying at the castle to economise.

Cynicus, of course, blamed the bank. About five years later he wrote *The Great Bank Fraud*. As a warning to businessmen it relates the treatment the Anderson family and the Company suffered at the hands of the North of Scotland Bank. He had pleaded with the general manager in Aberdeen to allow the business to continue. 'I spoke for the prosperity we had brought to the town, and for the work-people who had depended on me for so long. He finally consented; on one condition only. I must give the Bank another £1000 or a guarantee for that amount, or the Bank would take such steps as would probably "ruin you and your sisters".'

'One thousand pounds and only a week to find it!' Cynicus looked around for help. He was still waiting for his Surrey aunt's legacy and had been unable to raise money on it. The sisters in Scotland depended on him to rescue them all from penury. He would go to London in person. Besides, he had a private piece of business to transact there.

He bought a tourist ticket and stopped off at Leeds, where lived the Crockatts, wealthy cousins of the family that had taken in William in

Glasgow when the Anderson family split up. But the Crockatts did not offer cash.

Cynicus took a precious little case to a London pawnbroker.

I know a Bank when the wild time blows,
Where the Poet and the Painter and the Actor goes,
Where Orpheus takes his lute and Apollo takes his lyre,
Where the Artist takes his picture when he cannot find a buyer
And pop goes the easel.

Gems and other *objets de vertu* from the castle museum were turned into what he really needed, ready money. They were never redeemed. Even the gold signet ring he once wore is missing in later photographs.

In *The Great Bank Fraud* he phantasised about the London visit,

I set off for London, the scene of my early triumphs, the fair Bohemia of my youth, to become once more an unknown atom in the great Metropolis, to wander hopelessly among the phantoms of the past. I saw my work still everywhere displayed in the windows but it pained me indescribably... One afternoon I came upon a laughing crowd before a shop window filled with my pictures in the neighbourhood of Piccadilly Circus.

Unless some enterprising printseller was disposing of the Company's bankrupt stock it is hard to believe that this was not just a beautiful dream.

We do not know whether Martin met William and Nelly in London. The background to the rift between the brothers is confused and Cynicus intentionally kept it so, variously denying its existence and furnishing several versions. He placed it in 1900 (when William closed the studio), in 1904, and after the 1911 bankrupcy. Then he contradicted all the foregoing: 'I should like to make it clear that there has never been an open quarrel in the family or anything like it.' William in his one public

reference, placed the rupture in December 1904, when repayment of the Keary loan fell due. 'We have never spoken to each other since.'

The Leeds cousins assured him that the postcard industry was still flourishing in Yorkshire. 'They prevailed upon me... to go no further, but to start work again in their midst... So, after paying a call on some friends in London, I returned to Leeds and began once more.' A most diplomatic reference to his London mission.

With whatever he got for his treasures he returned to Fife to hearten his sisters. He persuaded the Glasgow Socialist paper *Forward* to print cartoons from *Cartoons Social and Political*. Then he tore himself away from his beloved castle and prepared to follow out his cousins' suggestion. He was already in Leeds, and the sisters in Tayport were trying to come to terms with their sudden ruin, when trouble struck again.

Marion lived with Lizzie, and William lived with Nelly, and John lived with Annie for a bit after The Grove became company property, but when Annie took up with her friends, the Misses Duncan, John withdrew to a house of his own and became a recluse. He had always been odd man out. Apprenticed to a seedsman when the family went to Glasgow, working as a freelance electrician in Tayport in 1891, described as an artist in 1902, he was clearly—in his own and in the family's eyes—a failure.

With horror Tayport learned in October 1912 that John, who had not been seen for six weeks, was lying dead in his house. His decomposed and unrecognisable body was found when worried neighbours summoned the police. The gaslight still burned in the kitchen; one newspaper of August date lay on the mat; the body was sprawled naked on the bathroom floor. Tayport buzzed with speculation. As, according to one version, he had told his sisters he was going away, he may have died of a heart attack as he stepped from his bath the evening before departure. The doctor who examined the remains guessed that death was from natural causes. One newspaper talked wildly of John's experiments with chemicals and the possibility of death by poison gas. He was fifty-five, reportedly 'very quiet, taking up with no one outside his own relations'. Lizzie grimly registered the death. John left only £127.

Leeds

The next stage in Cynicus's life, then, took place in Leeds. Three-quarters of an acre at Balmullo, accepted as security by John Crockatt of the Yorkshire Dyeworks, enabled him to set up the Cynicus Art Publishing Company at 52 Basinghall Street. Along the street at No. 20 was a department of the successful postcard publisher and printer, H G Glen & Co. As his cousin had pointed out, Yorkshire had still many colour printers and postcard manufacturers. Yet it is a pity that Cynicus could not see beyond postcards, now that that market was failing. He brought his salvaged blocks from Castle Cynicus to start re-issuing old designs, and also designed new motifs, no doubt relieved to be his own boss at last and resolved never to draw another love scene. He re-issued golf and holiday cards—'Our Holiday Start', 'Our Summer Quarters', 'Our Shooting Party', 'The Lovers Walk'—and such longstanding satirical favourites as 'A Lawsuit' and 'Wha Daur Meddle Wi' Me'.

There were enough light-hearted scenes, though, such as the merry picnic of old folk entitled 'Old Age Pension Day'. His crowded double-decker motorbus reappeared in Leeds; on 'The Last Boat' and 'The Last Train' and 'The Last Car' the masses still fought for room. He repeated the black and white 'reversible heads', pictures which become a different head when the card is turned upside down. 'Our Officer in Command' turns into a donkey. Since there was no Allan to stop him he brought out his favourite political cartoons again.

What was new? 'Our Aeroplane Express' is an aircraft as fanciful as his motorcars, with tophatted first-class passengers sitting on the wings,

1917?
PARIS AND BACK,
IN THREE HOURS.

second-class accommodated on swings below the fuselage, and third-class suspended in mid-air by the seats of their trousers.

In all, about a hundred cards have been traced with the Leeds company name on the back, but very few that have been through the post, and those bear mainly 1914 postmarks. Some of the unused cards are even unfinished; where the caption should be is only an empty space. Cynicus himself explained why, and it is the story of heartbreak.

'By the summer of 1914 I had published a lot of new work on a fine scale and was able to take a holiday at Castle Cynicus.' Poor Martin Anderson! Of course he sorely missed his castle. But Fate liked to award him a blow when he awarded himself a rest. The last time he finished a task and took a holiday was when he left London with *Cartoons Social and Political* awaiting review, and returned to find it had failed. Nor was this the last time.

While he was at Balmullo war broke out. Before he got back to Leeds a telegram from his cousin announced that he had paid off the workers and closed down the business. Suppressing all reference to the fury that must have possessed him Cynicus explained, 'It was a time when, fresh to the experience of a European conflict, people were apt to think an end had been put to the sale of everything but bare necessities.'

Thus was crushed the first brave attempt by the sixty-year-old to start again.

Chapter 15—'WAR!' and Peace 1915–21

UNDAUNTED BY CASUALTIES and conscription the nation cheered on the carnage. As Ramsay MacDonald remarked, 'No war is at first unpopular'. He was branded a traitor for advocating a negotiated peace. Keir Hardie died, disheartened by his failure to put down jingoism and worn out with overwork. Others of the old London crowd were flourishing. Conan Doyle went to the front as a war correspondent. Mrs Hodgson Burnett, Marie Corelli and Peggy Webling were churning out successful novels. Barrie had plays running to packed audiences.

Whether it was tenacity or desperation that drove him, Cynicus made another new start. This time he went to Edinburgh—like Leeds, a city where he had next to no contacts. James Marchbank, a solicitor with Balmullo connections, gave him a lease of the semi-basement shop below his own office at the east end of York Place. York Place is a continuation of Queen Street, the solicitors' quarter. At that time the east end debouched into the slums at the top of Leith Walk; with its street walkers and Saturday night fights and Theatre Royal it was not unlike the Drury Lane milieu.

For a reason that will soon appear the postcards produced from 45 York Place were few. A few cards from Leeds were overprinted with the new Edinburgh address, a few topical captions were added to old designs. Against his principles and out of necessity, he published one or two patriotic cards for other people. The aeroplane card got a hopeful new caption that imagined a peaceful future in '1917? Paris and Back in Three Hours'.

He found staff for the shop and retired to the castle to write *The Great Bank Fraud,* his bitter attack on the banking system that had ruined him. It was published at his York Place studio, at the 'War Price' of one shilling. But once again he suffered unforeseen disaster. For yet again he was not on the spot when needed. The printing blocks arrived from Leeds. 'The people in Edinburgh sold them, though they were worth hundreds of pounds, for scrap metal.' He did not explain whether 'the people' were merely stupid, whether they were helping the salvage drive, or whether they were paying themselves overdue wages. 'I am now sixty-one,' he wrote privately, 'and it seems that every loophole is being stopped and that I shall be stifled out of life.' 'There was only one thing for me to do and that was to start all over again... I felt myself a complete stranger in Edinburgh.'

133

This time there were no employees. Cynicus was his own shopkeeper. The customer who opened the glass door decorated with the insignia, 'Truth the Lyre', found himself in a narrow passage lined with artist's materials propped against the wall. To the left was the front shop, hung with prints. Ahead lay the tiny backshop where he slept, cooked his frugal meal, and shared it with an adopted alley cat. In surroundings reminiscent of his London studio he proposed to make history repeat itself.

How to arrest the attention of the passersby? What was contentious now? In common with most ordinary people, he had been stunned that a Balkan incident in 1914 could set off a chain reaction of pledges and land Britain in a world war. Unlike most he was not cheering on the latest massacre of youth. During the Drury Lane discussions Hardie and MacDonald had condemned nineteenth century British imperialism—war waged in the Crimea, China, Ethiopia, Ashanti, Afghanistan, Zululand and the Sudan till a third of the world's population paid tribute to London. Since then, as Cynicus pointed out in *Who Shall Rule?* the Boer War had claimed twenty thousand lives to capture the Rand goldfields for plutocracy. Now the battle of the Somme had claimed twenty thousand in a day. For what? As MacDonald said, 'You can win the war; and in winning it pay such a price that the nation will have lost.'

He put all his anger into a great poster entitled 'WAR!' and placed it in his window. To court publicity Cynicus did not need to compromise his ideals. War is ruled by Mammon. Crowds worship him, Lust caresses him. Justice and Parliament stand bound, while the Church encourages the slaughter and the Banks snatch unclaimed savings from the dead. In the foreground a bloody river bears the young men away.

In a 1958 article in the *Scottish Daily Express* Albert Mackie confessed that this cartoon made a lifelong impression on him. He could not forget the head of a boy crying for his mother as he drowned. It made such an impression on so many people that a policeman friend of Cynicus feared the authorities were about to invoke DORA against him. Under the terms of DORA (Defence of the Realm Act) agitators could be indefinitely interned without trial. PC Paterson prevailed on the artist to remove 'WAR!' from the shop window before its creator was incarcerated. He was persuaded to display non-political subjects instead. He still made postcards of 'WAR!' and sold them in the shop.

His old shop window stratagem had succeeded all the same. His audacity had captured attention, brought him new contacts, and given him a lifeline in a strange city. Soon his social life, if not so brilliant and brisk as it had been in London, was opening up new possibilities. He began to paint, not just pictures for sale but small landscapes on board as gifts for the friends he made—some with the same romantically spiky mountains, rosy glow and stags of earlier days, some in the calm, pure colours of his other style. He was pleased with both.

'A Land Fit for Heroes'

As a Victorian, Cynicus had misgivings about the postwar world. The best of the nation had been wiped out, the survivors were the disabled and unfit, and luxury and unnatural hours were weakening them further. He deplored the craze for novelty, the restless rush for excitement, the preoccupation with racing, gambling and football, for these were all distractions provided by Mammon to fend off the threat of class war. He was pleased that the people were abandoning the Church. In his final book, *Through Wisdom's Glasses,* he accuses the Church of driving the sheep to slaughter. It 'tore the command "Thou shalt not kill" from the Decalogue, but "Vengeance is mine, saith the Lord", and the position of the church today shows He remembers.'

To express his disgust at the state of the nation he drew another outspoken political poster, 'The Dictator'. The war survivors have returned to what was promised to be a 'land fit for heroes'. They find awaiting them instead Lloyd George, The Showman, with Marconi shares sticking out of his pocket and Broken Pledges underfoot; and the Church, with full round belly; holding between them a banner inscribed 'Britain's Welcome to the Troops'. But it frames the Poorhouse door. A begging soldier labelled 'Glory in the Gutter' says: 'I have served my country And this is how my country serves me.' At a dead soldier's feet are the words: 'I died for Liberty and Freedom And they are dead for whom I died.' He lies before the graves of Britain's Honour and Liberty. In the foreground another soldier holds a paper of Government Promises. The caption reads 'Alas! my dear dead comrade of the line, The war that closed your eyes has opened mine.'

The background is filled by the fat figure of Capitalism seated on great sacks of Labour's Earnings, using the Press to blast out Falsehood and Misrepresentation, setting the Black and Tans on Ireland, and threatening Labour—but giant Labour wields a cudgel marked Strike.

At the end of the Great War the men came home to a country that had not yet readjusted to peace time production. In the traditional phrase, 'too much money was chasing too few goods', and prices rocketed. In 1920 price increases were at their peak. Slump followed boom, and money was scarce again.

The family racked its brains for ways to make Castle Cynicus pay and to keep their brother going in Edinburgh. He for his part did his best to drum up paying guests for Castle Cynicus. Annie moved out from Tayport with her friend Miss Duncan and worked hard cooking on a coal

136

range and—since the plumbing had never been completed—lugging in water for cooking, washing and laundry. With its huge studio cum ballroom, Castle Cynicus had been designed for large-scale entertaining, but not for overnight guests. The septuagenarian Annie not only had to be housekeeper for the lodgers, but often give up her bedroom. As she confided to Lizzie, the guests were not always grateful.

Marion and Lizzie, the Tayport sisters, collected pieces of cloth to make into curtains, since as much space as possible was to serve as sleeping accommodation. Lizzie's letters to Annie at Balmullo reveal the poverty that gripped the entire family. Marion unpicked the skirt of an old dress so that Annie could re-use the material. Lizzie sent mildewed remnants from the shop. Gradually the castle was deteriorating. There was no money for repairs to the roof. Since gutters and downpipes had not all been fitted, rainwater cascaded down the walls and made the interior ever damper. As the years passed, the once fine furnishings became shabby. Nothing that wore out was replaced.

Alarmed that he might go bankrupt and lose the castle, Martin bonded it to its full value for fictional loans from his three Fife sisters, thus making them preferential creditors if it came to the worst.

In Edinburgh, meanwhile, he had gathered around him a host of new friends. All his life he had joined or instituted clubs and societies, and Edinburgh was no different. He revived the Athenian Club, a literary society where members read out their work and had it criticised; he became its president. There were meetings, lectures and dinners of the Fabians and the Independent Labour Party and he made friends among them. That genial personality of his was coming to his aid as ever. He was commissioned to paint a banner, for which Lizzie hoped he had 'got a satisfactory arrangement'. Now and again he painted a portrait, but was in no position to command much of a fee.

Save the Castle

He and his new friends hatched a plan to put the castle's finances on a better footing. He had always said it was to be open to the public at all times for rest, recreation and education, and on his death it would become public property, as a college for the workers or a convalescent home. Why wait? Let it become public property now and give Martin and Annie a job as resident caretakers. If the fabric were looked after they could live on a ten shilling pension and garden produce.

After a wave of disasters Cynicus always bobbed up again. His inextinguishable optimism reasserted itself at the slightest sign that could possibly be interpreted as an improvement. 'The best is to be. The best is happening now.' Wilful blindness or wisdom kept him faithful to this motto. In February 1921 he was bubbling with enthusiasm when his friends set up a committee and concocted the 'Castle Cynicus Scheme'. They elected an Honorary Treasurer and an Honorary Secretary, and asked Annie to draw up a list of people who might respond to a circular. In May the leading lights met at the castle to plan the launch of the Scheme. In June they sent out their circular. Since bedrooms in the castle were so few the illustration imaginatively added another wing discreetly tucked behind trees. The letterpress announced:

> Castle Cynicus and its grounds, situated in the Parish of Leuchars, Fifeshire, having been placed gratuitously at the service of the public in the surrounding area for close on twenty years, Cynicus, the owner, being desirous of extending the benefits as a holiday resort to all workers, men and women, irrespective of creed, sect, or party, is handing over the entire estate to a Committee of Management to carry out his proposed scheme. The policy of this scheme will be Educational, on such lines as will promote the highest interests of the worker and further the cause of Peace and Goodwill among men. It will not be a charity in any sense, but will be entirely self-supporting.

The Reverend William Marwick, the Organising Secretary, might seem a surprising colleague for Cynicus in this scheme, being a former missionary, but he was a fervent Labour supporter.

Marwick was organising a fête to inaugurate the scheme in July. As the promotion leaflet confidently announced, it was 'intended to have Sports and Highland Games as an annual event'. Cynicus had presented ten pictures for a raffle, valued [by him?] at £15 each, and Annie persuaded her sisters and friends to sell books of tickets. A stall at the fête would sell cartoons to those disappointed in the raffle. He wrote to Annie from the shop, with customary optimism:

> I have quite a show in my window now & am still busy with more. They are attracting much attention but tho I have a good many promises I have made no definite sales yet. I have spent all my spare cash on Frames & if you can send me 5/- to keep things going on Temporarily I'll be very glad. Such is Life! To see the grand show in my window you'd think I must be well-to-do. However that will be all right later.

But Lizzie pointed out how doubtful the financial climate was: 'I hope by the time for your sale comes round that the miners will be back at work and the other workers on full time. As we know in the meantime there is very little money to spare.' The miners' lockout did not end till August.

Excitement was at fever pitch when there was a last-minute scare over the legality of the raffle tickets; the official who heard their case recollected that his wife had danced with Cynicus at a ball in the castle, and ruled the raffle bona-fide.

Lizzie injected her usual note of gloom: 'We are too much troubled as to how we are to pay our business debts ever to think of adding to our troubles by running into debt for clothes. Marion's purple dress and light coat are fairly passable and we are to try to scrape the price of a hat for her.'

The garden fête was a great success, the *Dundee Advertiser* reporting:

> People from the surrounding districts turned out in force, and the woodland charms of the Castle grounds were explored by eager crowds. The opening ceremony was performed by Lord Cardross, who was introduced by the Rev. Wm Marwick, of Edinburgh. The sports were held in a field adjoining the Castle, and evoked much interest.

Someone had dug out an ancient Conservative Black Rod to lend conventional respectability to the Socialist scene. It was Lord Cardross's last public engagement.

It did look as if the Andersons' luck had turned at last, but they were unable to look back with pleasure on what should have been their moment of triumph. The day was blighted. The reason for Lizzie's anxiety to 'scrape the price of a hat' for her sister's day out was that Marion was suffering from myxodoema, which dulls the mind, puffs up the body and causes loss of hair. Overtaxed by excitement, she suffered a stroke. Three weeks later she died.

In 1909, when her Company shares were worth something, Marion had made a will in Lizzie's favour. Lizzie tried to get her brother to repay outstanding loans—in vain, of course. Marion's estate, including her Surrey aunt's legacy of shares, amounted to only £167.

As for William Martin's bequest of eight or nine properties to the Andersons, it had gradually disappeared. Since the mortgage interest was not kept up, the houses were repossessed one after another and sold to pay off arrears. The erosion of the family's inheritance went on till everything William Martin had left his widow and daughters passed into the hands of the building society; and when the properties were sold off there was not a penny left for the family.

Henceforward Lizzie bore Martin a grudge. The family alliance was crumbling.

The earliest lesson we learn by heart,
Is *how to take each other's part.*

139

Chapter 16—A Knock-out Blow 1921–28

MARTIN, HOWEVER, brushed aside such dismal considerations and looked to a rosy future. The old Victorian had developed some typical postwar characteristics. He 'noted with pride and joy the glorious type of young manhood we have with us today who have been taught that: Self denied Pride ruled and Duty satisfied Are better far than Pleasure gratified. He stands for everything noble and true and we hear his clear ringing voice telling us all "Your time today, 'Tis mine tomorrow!"'

Britain was full of men and women who believed that the young could be redeemed by the great out-of-doors, plain living and high thinking, regular hours and fresh air, Socialism or scouting. Cynicus visualised his castle doing good to city boys and unemployed miners. A book collection was donated to help kit out his rural education centre. These books ended their lives in the castle as torn leaves scattered over the floor.

They had really turned the corner at last, he felt. The Workers' Institute in Abercromby Place became the venue for more fund-raising. The artist was to give a series of lectures with demonstrations and advice on oil painting and sketching from nature at a shilling a time.

In May 1922 the Castle Cynicus Scheme organised a picnic to Balmullo. But that seems to be the sum total of its efforts to keep the castle going. In September the Athenian Club booked a weekend. Martin brightened up and wrote to Annie:

> There's nothing like keeping the place going. I had a visit from the two Millars last night on the subject of charges. I first mentioned 15/- ea. but saw that was more than they cd entertain. Finally I told them it wd be 10/- ea. if 20 came & £12 even if more than 20 came. The lady hasn't turned up again about the cottage. Another lady called last night & wanted it for one week in July. I said it wd be 30/- for one week. You didn't say if you had got cups. I see them here now at 2d ea. Things are v. slow here at present but hope they will brighten soon. Hoping you do good biz with the visitors tomorrow.

The problem was always where to stow the visitors and boarders, yet families gladly put up with the rustic inconveniences and cramped sleeping accommodation. Martin wrote to Annie that a family with young baby would come for a month and do all the work and pay fifteen shillings a week in exchange for her room and a bed in the library. This would allow Annie away for a holiday. Cynicus corrected himself on the last point. If she came to York Place for a time it would help him 'to get the business started again', for, he concluded, 'The prospects are improving every day'.

But the struggle continued unabated. An Athenian, happening to call in at York Place one day, found him almost in tears over a final demand from the electricity company for £2.10/-. To the artist living on a few shillings a week such a demand was overwhelming.

May 1924 was a better month than many. True, Lizzie, still looking for Marion's loan to be repaid, sent a letter 'full of spite and malignity', but on the positive side two picnic parties were arranged for June, and Cynicus proposed to spend a week at the castle to entertain the first group and welcome the next. He rightly felt that what brought them to Balmullo was the entertainment. Also, he was to receive payment for a portrait and told Annie he would be 'all right for June at any rate'. He was wrong, for June brought fresh calamity.

Cynicus and a friend went out visiting one evening in Edinburgh. They prolonged enjoyable conversation till a late hour. Then Cynicus walked home. At the National Gallery he was stopped by his policeman friend and told the terrible news that fire had broken out in the studio. While he was cracking jokes with his friends two fire engines had

[Courtesy of N.E. Fife District Museum Service]

been pouring water into the semi-basement. Cynicus and the constable hurried to the scene. He opened the door. Inside 'there was nothing but blackness and ruin. The place was streaming with water and black with dirt and smoke. Many of my pictures and books were destroyed.' Needless to say, they were not insured.

The firemaster estimated the extent of the damage for his report. To him the whole stock of the studio was worth no more than £200, and the loss was only £10, with another £5 for repairs to the fabric. To the seventy-year-old artist, though, it meant the end. He had not the means to redecorate or even to make the blackened backshop habitable again. Fate had administered the *coup de grâce*.

Friends salvaged what they could. Cynicus toiled upstairs to Marchbank and gave up the tenancy. It seemed he was broken at last. Perhaps he was relieved that the struggle was over. There was now no place left for him but Castle Cynicus. There he and Annie and Miss Duncan could pool their ten shilling pensions and continue to live.

A fine-art restorer took over the shop, and let the poor old fellow use it as an accommodation address. He was soon displaying the cartoons in his window. Cynicus resumed his role as entertainer, but his heart was sore. He found it impossible to repeat, 'The best is now. The best is yet to be.' He sat down one evening after a concert at the castle, took a salvaged sheet of Cynicus Publishing Company paper, and wrote out neatly the following cry of anguish:

16th Dec 24.

I write these few words for future eyes to read. Tonight things look blacker than they ever did in all my tragic life. The hand of Fate seems to hold me with an iron grasp & is crushing me down. How little the happy people who tonight enjoyed my songs & laughter imagined that all that made life for me is being taken from me & yet how small a sum would retrieve all. My pictures lie neglected & unsold—my food for the last 6 weeks has cost less than 6d per day, & yet with all my sacrifice and self denial I am getting deeper and deeper in the quicksands with no one to lend a helping hand—How long O Lord how long?

Cynicus.

He had maintained his public mask of good cheer, his 'fatal smile', all evening. But the brave story in *The Great Bank Fraud,* of seeing his pictures in London printshops, of laughing crowds applauding them, fell away when he addressed posterity. 'My pictures lie neglected and unsold.'

The Edinburgh friend who had paid the York Place electricity bill was invited to stay at the castle and reminded in advance there were no shops nearby. He was glad he arrived well provided with food, for there was little to eat on the premises.

'Wayland Smith' of the *Daily Record,* who had known Cynicus since about 1917, remarked that he was becoming difficult to get on with as he aged, and yet one was willing to be patient with him because he was a lovable little person and an undoubted genius. Small wonder if a man so continuously buffeted by Fate should eventually become difficult to get on with.

Once he left Edinburgh, no more was heard of the Castle Cynicus Scheme. According to 'Wayland Smith': 'Nothing ever came of it because of his obstinacy in refusing to get down to what people call "brass tacks", and because of the error he made in roping in to his committee almost every crank in Edinburgh.' Martin's character contained the fatal conjunction of suggestibility and obstinacy.

Yet even now he was not ready to submit. In November 1925 he wrote to his former friend, Ramsay MacDonald, now Prime Minister, and asked him to read his latest work and recommend it to a publisher. *Through Wisdom's Glasses* was a series of essays composed over the years, with an introduction written after the war. The introduction is in the form of a fairytale. Wisdom visits Cynicus in his tower bedroom during the War, attracted, he says mischievously, by a chink in the defective blackout curtains, and leaves the spectacles that give him wisdom. The essays range over time and space, geology and theology and evolution, life and death, youth and war, law and money. These were largely random jottings put down as they occurred to him. A few are marred by tiresome repetition of a motif. Others are original and well argued. All betray the self-indulgence of the private journal rather than the incisiveness of the earlier pamphlets. His forte was the one-liner or the couplet. Firing off shots all round he had difficulty in keeping to the point for the length of an essay.

Cynicus had had virtually no contact with Ramsay MacDonald for decades. In his letter he adopted a masterful tone, perhaps the final echo of those exhilarating Drury Lane days, when his ebullient personality drew crowds of admirers. The Premier was informed that the manuscript dealt 'with great questions of the day from an entirely new point of view' and 'if you shewed it to your friends and Colleagues, I feel sure they would be unanimous to have it published at once'. He enclosed a sample poem:

The Courtier

Would you rise to high estate
Seek the favours of the great:
Keep your counsel, watch and wait,
Flatter and conciliate.
Learn to creep and crawl and cringe.
In your backbone have a hinge.
Keep your conscience in your pocket,

Your honour in a drawer and lock it.
Whatsoever thing you try
Do it with a single I.
Strive still to attain your end
Even though it cost a friend.
That is how the game is played.
That is how the Courtier's made.

MacDonald replied kindly and did try to help. He sent the manuscript to the publisher Jonathan Cape, who turned it down. When Cynicus next offered to donate Castle Cynicus to 'the Cause', the Prime Minister suggested approaching the Workers' Educational Association. In April 1926 Cynicus dropped the bluff. The castle was on the verge of being sold off to repay debts. In desperation he sent the Premier a begging letter. 'Can you, by me formally handing over to you all my Library and Museum for the benefit of the working men for all time, *temporarily* grant me the use of One hundred pounds?' On the 24th, just after his 72nd birthday, he pleaded outright for £100 'to obviate disaster'. He could offer a shilling book of all his Labour cartoons, 'ready to print off', for sixpence wholesale. Or he could write weekly articles for a newspaper. Rumour has it that Cynicus did receive £100 from Ramsay MacDonald. At all events the castle was saved.

By mid-1926 Annie and he had devised a new plan. Yet again headed writing paper was procured, this time for The Cynicus Publishing Company, Castle Cynicus, Balmullo. Once Cynicus left Edinburgh he finally lost the will to paint and sought outlet for his feelings in a cheaper medium, print.

First he published a second edition of *The Great Bank Fraud*. A letter from the company's 'manager' requested a review in the Socialist paper *Forward*. Since the paper was engaged in promoting the Co-op Bank it naturally ignored this request. He also published a small pamphlet entitled *No.40 Dixie's Land*. It purports to be a contribution to the Land for the People movement, but fires indiscriminately at various targets. It sets out to expose the profit made from renting out tenement flats in Glasgow, Dixie's Land being a row of tenements (once called 'lands' in Scotland). This pamphlet bears no printer's name or date, contains a good few misprints, and was published at Castle Cynicus. Its diffuse repetitiveness is most unlike the clear hardhitting style of a work like *The Great Bank Fraud*. Inside the back cover was an advertisement for the *Satires of Cynicus,* to be published shortly, price one shilling.

In due course this fifth and final edition of the *Satires* was printed by Dundee Printers Ltd and published by Cynicus Publishing Company, Castle Cynicus. From the aesthetic point of view it is a lamentable production, with two hundred sketches jammed together on sixty pages regardless of contrasting scales. Yet in the circumstances it was an achievement to publish at all, and for Cynicus it was a way to vent in print the feelings he could never express aloud. For the old sketches, mostly

[Courtesy of N.E. Fife District Museum Service]

those first published in 1890, are reproduced in a sequence that is a veiled commentary on Cynicus's own life. The author is exploited; the Church is pharisaical and grasping; law and politics likewise; Labour is exploited; money is a necessity and a curse; marriage is a mistake; fame is evanescent; poverty alienates friends; debt shackles Prometheus. After 'IOU' comes the couplet

The merry Fool in motley at the Fair
May hide in jest and laughter his despair.

By page 45 he has reached the end of his cryptic confession with 'Memento Mori'. As makeweight he throws in a miscellany of further favourites, and examples from two forthcoming books that would never see the light—*Humours of Cynicus* and *Through Wisdom's Glasses*. The new *Humours* would have been another shilling book of cartoons and postcards, ruined by the necessity for a cut-price format. The very last page is dedicated to one small picture. Stones and old boots rain on the man who dared to tell the world the truth—himself.

After this last burst of publishing in 1926 Cynicus devoted himself to 'my Earthworks and my Book'. Repeatedly he put the finishing touches to the Book (*Through Wisdom's Glasses*). As for his earthworks, he had undertaken the ambitious task of making a walk up to the house from the road that passed the foot of his land. A newspaper article would later mention his 'solo performance, a job that any young man would probably flee the country rather than undertake, for its course runs over the roughest of ground, with boulders and whin bushes among the obstacles. He has been at the job now for two and a half years, has made roughly 150 yards, and during the time has laid down 12,000 barrowfuls of material.' He worked on it up to the last.

Annie's friend Miss Duncan stayed on as unpaid housekeeper to look after the lodgers. As she served breakfast to them all Cynicus remarked mildly, 'My egg's cracked.' To the delight of a young guest she countered with, 'Aye, there's mair than that cracked here.'

It might be concluded that old age was sapping his mental powers. That was soon proved wrong. There was a last triumph yet to come.

He shall have hate and scorn, in sooth,
Who dares to tell the World the truth.

Chapter 17—Cynicus Rediscovered 1928–30

AT CHRISTMAS 1928 an Edinburgh friend sent them a chicken. Cynicus was pathetically grateful and sent him in return the best he had to give, a copy of the 1890 *Satires*. They had only one visitor in the house over Hogmanay, though they had hosted a Curlers' Dance the night before. At Hogmanay 1929 they had several visitors, and one was a journalist who had come specifically to interview Cynicus. Within a day or two there were reports in the *Sunday Express,* the *Sunday Mail,* the *Daily Record,* the *Glasgow Evening News,* the *People's Journal* and the *Courier & Advertiser.* Suddenly the public was once more interested in Cynicus.

The journalist who arrived at Castle Cynicus on New Year's Eve gave one of the last descriptions of that mansion and its occupants. He was enchanted with Cynicus—'as quaint and lovable a personality as any stranger could meet', while Annie '— sister and guardian angel of her brother—gave the assurance of a hearty welcome'. She left the visitor in the great studio to fetch Cynicus from his den below. Looking about him, the reporter noted a pipe organ, grand piano, walls covered in Cynicus's own canvases and sketches, 'state vases, magnificent ornaments, and rare curios' under a lofty decorated ceiling.

The host arrived.

Clad in grey tweeds, on top of which was an ancient coat, his features were reflected from a tiny paraffin lamp he carried in his left hand. Peering through his glasses with his face aglow in warm friendship, he reciprocated the season's greetings...

"Ah!" he exclaimed, "if only you had come an hour ago, this Liberty Hall rang with the laughter of children making merry." With the miniature light held aloft he led the way through the Gallery and Entrance Hall—with its quaint furnishings—to a winding staircase, at the foot of which Cynicus was "at Home in his Den"! There for hours we sat and chatted—rather he did the talking and I the listening.

No more romantic setting could be imagined for a New Year's Night. The stormy winds could blow outside—here by the hearth and under the soft glow of the lamp Cynicus unfolded his "life".

Squatted in his favourite easy chair, with his sister at the opposite side of the hearth, Cynicus certainly belied his years. If the hair and head are not so cavalier as of old... his is still indeed a striking figure.

At Castle Cynicus, January 1930
[Courtesy of N.E. Fife District Museum Service]

Forty years after the *Sketch* interview in London, Cynicus could still twist the interviewer round his little finger. In his late seventies he was still being thought young for his years.

Vain about his appearance, he grew his remaining hair long and brushed it over his bald crown; for a picture he always removed his pince-nez and presented the profile. It was still a handsome little head. The forehead was smooth, the short-sighted eyes were clear and innocent. With his lifelong bias towards looking on the bright side he was only half in fun when he imagined his glasses had endowed him with wisdom.

Before long, he was reading to the interviewer from *Through Wisdom's Glasses*. 'He read chapter after chapter—brimful of his whimsical humour and well seasoned with sage advice.' The evening was rounded off by the host playing the organ and piano and singing with other guests.

Cynicus gave his opinion of contemporary cartoonists: 'Their work is only for the day—they are out of date in a week. My "story" is permanent and that was the secret of my success.'

One must admire those old stagers Annie and Martin, as they put a brave face on their reduced circumstances, not seeking a sympathetic hearing for a tale of woe but minimising their distress. They would rather not make visitors uncomfortable. They had been exuding good fellowship for decades.

A Mysterious Affair

The sudden interest in Cynicus originated in an article put out by the *Sunday Express* on the twenty-ninth of December. It was a touching story headed 'Two Brothers'.

> A disagreement between two brothers a quarter of a century ago still keeps them apart. One of the brothers is Mr. William Anderson, of... Southend, and the other is Mr. Martin Anderson, who as "Cynicus" was a noted artist of a generation ago... The elder brother broke down when I visited him dreaming by the fireside of that unfortunate quarrel. "I am afraid our next meeting will not be in this world. We are both too old to travel."

Now, this is a most mysterious affair. Who put the *Sunday Express* on to William?

In April the Glasgow *Daily Record & Mail* had run a paragraph on the death of Fenton Mackay, a Dundonian who enjoyed a brief vogue in 1898 as a London playwright. It went on to describe the Drury Lane studio where he had been a guest. In September the Dundee *Evening Telegraph* had published an interview, entitled 'The Premier's Fife Friend', all about Cynicus in London. *Through Wisdom's Glasses* was not the only writing Cynicus had been engaged on. He had his memoirs all ready for publication. What he still needed was publicity.

It looks as if a strenuous effort to publicise him was being made in Scotland. In England another paper copied the *Sunday Express* story and ladled on the pathos:

> One of the loneliest men in England this Christmas was Mr William Anderson, brother of "Cynicus". He broke down completely... when a Press representative... found him alone in the solitude of his little room... he was dreaming of an unfortunate day when he and his brother disagreed... 'We have never spoken to each other since,' he sobbed, pitifully... There was no enmity whatever in the old man's voice, only regret. He looked into the fire again; then his eyes sparkled with pride as he reflected on his brother's gifts.

Then the *People's Journal* reported:

> The public imagination has been touched by the old man calling to his brother over the miles which divide them, and interest has been heightened by the discovery that the brother thus addressed... is "Cynicus", the famous artist and cartoonist of a former generation, and the inventor of the comic postcard.

No doubt many had thought Cynicus long dead. On Friday 4th January it was his turn to get into the papers. He gave a garbled account of the quarrel with William, then swiftly seized the opportunity to present himself. 'One result of the publicity given to the case of my brother and myself has been very pleasing to me... It has shown me that I am not so much in the background as I had supposed... I have long since stopped making sketches for the press, but I have drawn over 200 illustrations for a book which I am at present writing.'

The next day he answered a ring at the front door. On the doorstep stood a smiling reporter.

Behind him—Cynicus fell back astounded—stood William.

'Is it really you Willie?' he gasped.

Each, to his surprise, saw an old man. William was eighty, Martin seventy-five. Martin saw a dapper little figure with cane, spats and highly polished shoes. William saw a small crumpled person in a shabby suit and carpet slippers.

The reporter had to admit it was 'a tense greeting'. He suggested an outdoor photograph. Cynicus eagerly led the way without stopping to put on his overcoat. William doucely followed. The brothers posed at the sundial, where William managed a cadaverous smile and Martin took off his glasses and gazed into the distance. Snow swirled briefly and drove them back to the house. They trooped silently up to the ballroom where Annie awaited them.

Determined to give his readers a happy story, the reporter jotted it down:

> While I am writing this, the two brothers and their sister, whose combined ages total 238 years, are somewhere within the castle walls, revelling in

their newly-found happiness... They were sitting by the fireside, their faces aglow and their minds wandering happily back down the avenues of time. Each is reminding the other of days that are gone, while in the armchair in the corner sits their smiling maiden sister Annie... It is the happiest New Year of their lives.

A photo shows their faces anything but aglow. William, having rashly removed his overcoat, has been lent a thick dressing-gown to keep out the chill; he bends towards Annie with a timidly ingratiating half-smile; Annie, sitting opposite, watches him bleakly; Cynicus, 'making the most of his inches', leans against the mantlepiece without his spectacles, gazing unseeing into the distance, the picture of embarrassment.

The surprise reunion did not in fact lead to reconciliation. The 4th of January article in the *People's Journal* had quoted 'an intimate friend' of William's as saying, 'I have known Mr Anderson, who is a Broughty Ferry man, for a considerable number of years, and he has always been exceedingly sensitive about the incidents which have just been disclosed.' Fortunately William would have had no opportunity to see the newspapers that day, one of which reported Cynicus as saying, 'It is most cruel. My brother and I are friendly, in fact we are in correspondence regularly, and I heard from him only the other day.' Clearly William was not the only one 'exceedingly sensitive about the incidents'.

Perhaps the reporter allowed William to make the short trip to Tayport to call on Lizzie. Since over the years it was she who had remained in contact with him he was no doubt keen to see her again, possibly keener to visit Lizzie than to meet Martin and Annie. He knew she was on her own, bedridden and near her end. When Martin visited her house just three weeks later it was to register her death.

The publicity given to the story sheds a little light on William's life since the death of Nelly's husband in 1912. Since Andersons always stuck together, he and Nelly had continued to live together in Holborn till she died of pneumonia fourteen years later, in June 1926. Then William was left quite alone in London. He now occupied a couple of rooms in a Southend boarding house.

'I have remained a bachelor,' he told the *Sunday Express,* 'because at the time of life when I might have married I had too many other responsibilities. My only visitor now is Mr Moffat, the minister of Crown Court Church, Drury Lane.'

The report continued: 'Mr. Anderson is a university in himself. He has more than a thousand books in his room, and, in addition to speaking seven languages, there is hardly a subject of which he is not thoroughly well-informed. He was a linguist in the censor's office during the war.'

Annie, Martin and Willie meet, January 1930 [Courtesy of N.E. Fife District Museum Service]

William returned to Southend and again faded from sight.

Cynicus, on the other hand, had been rediscovered. He had used every opportunity to advertise his forthcoming book; he was doing all in his power to claw his way back from obscurity. He sent thanks to the *Sunday Express.* He gave interviews to the *Sunday Mail,* the *Daily Record,* and the *Glasgow Evening News.* The last agreed to run his memoirs in instalments, and almost every week he sent some snippet to the Talk of the Town column to keep interest alive until the reminiscences appeared. In early February Talk of the Town declared that he was 'reaping the benefit of the recent publicity that took place over the reconciliation with his brother. Grant Richards... are to publish a book of his shortly, "Through Wisdom's Glasses," and I understand that about the beginning of April he will broadcast from Edinburgh.' By March 5th it was clear that Grant Richards had rejected the book. Cynicus was now keen to publish in Glasgow, as a favour to the city that had first appreciated him. There was a paragraph about building his own road, and a day or two later a report that he had sent Ramsay MacDonald a song called 'International Song of Peace'. (The premier had just concluded an Anglo-American agreement to limit armaments.)

The 'Memoirs of Cynicus' appeared in the *Glasgow Evening News* in twelve instalments during February and March 1930. *The Daily Record & Mail* also printed one excerpt of particular interest to its Glasgow readers—the inception of the St Mungo Art Club. Cynicus retold his life, enlivening it with quaint anecdotes, dwelling on the bright moments, hastening past his misfortunes. On the same principle, when it came to individuals he had decided 'to keep my mouth firmly shut. Of those whom I hold in regard you shall hear; of those others, with whose mentality I was or am at variance, you shall hear nothing but the echo of their names.' '*Am* at variance,' be it noted. Not quite true, for he devoted a whole instalment to Keary's nouveau riche pretensions, with a parting shot at Keary's colleague Sir Arthur Pearson. Though Pearson was dear to the public as the founder of St Dunstan's Home for the Blind when he went blind himself, Cynicus dwelled on his unsuccessful effort to buy a peerage. Of William, though, he said not a word, either of blame for his London mistakes or of gratitude for his sacrifice of his own career to help Mother's favourite.

The memoirs opened with a restatement of his philosophy of art, unaltered through almost forty years: 'Brevity is the soul of wit. It was my earliest endeavour by elimination to oust the unnecessary line, to take away that which obscured and to discover that minimum that suggested in itself all that I intended to convey.'

Either he or the sub-editor skilfully tailored the memoirs to suit the readership. They began with his Glasgow youth, omitted anything controversial in his politics and included pointless anecdotes about royalty. Whole numbers were devoted to extrovert anecdotes about other people. The old entertainer still wore his cheerful mask. He carefully hid the negative side of his personality, even on occasions when it would have been justifiable to complain. He cannot have realised how he gave away his egotism when he related incidents involving other members of the family as if they referred to himself, such as the Portuguese who gave language lessons at Guardbridge. The silences are eloquent. Where one might expect an account of failure he would relate a trifling success. In 1894, rather than face the fact that *Cartoons Social and Political* failed he concentrated on a one-off commission from the umbrella-maker 'Drooko' Wright. He reported that H W Massingham, editor of the *Daily Chronicle,* said in 1899 'Now you are up and I am down', whereas we know that both were down, Massingham because he had lost his job and Cynicus because he had lost his livelihood. He deflected attention from the company's difficulties in 1910 by relating the marked attention paid him in public by his guest Harry Lauder. The only clouds allowed to appear in the sunny landscape were the auction of his pictures and the York Place fire.

The 'Memoirs of Cynicus' aroused considerable interest. Names from the past wrote in to add detail, such as John Hassall, or to dispute details, such as James Greig and Mrs Keary; locals wrote in to add stories relevant to Glasgow, or to mention just as strange coincidences that had befallen them; an enterprising artshop made a window display of Cynicus prints.

The gossip column reported in March that some friends had petitioned for a Civil List pension for Cynicus:

> Various financial misfortunes beginning as far back as 1912 have seriously affected his well-being and although he still retains Castle Cynicus it is at the cost of the most rigid economy. It has been felt by the friends, and by many others, that the nation owes something to this man who with his pen and pencil so flagellated the follies and injustices of his time.

It would have made such a difference to his last years of life if he had had just a little extra, but it did not come off. Perhaps the 'friends' were just Annie and himself. Yet so many of his old acquaintances were now wealthy.

Cynicus ended his memoirs with the philosophy of life, which, like his philosophy of art, had sustained him through the years: 'Everything is for the best, and my prayer every morning and evening is: "The best has happened, the best is going to happen, and the best is happening now." I have never found it to fail, and I can recommend it to anyone who cares to prove it.' Happy self- deception.

Since Cynicus had been discovered to be a raconteur with a store of entertaining anecdotes the BBC asked him to give a talk in their 'I Remember' series. He broadcast from the Edinburgh studio on a Saturday evening in April. When he had duly denounced the bank that ruined him he returned home delighted to have told the world the truth, only to discover that the BBC had faded him out at that point. However, he was paid for the talk and that was a consolation.

Some days later his life-long friend Bob Graham in the throes of bronchitis breathed his last. There is no record of how it affected him.

Brightened though it was by public interest in his life the daily grind of poverty remained. A summer school was held at the castle, the participants sleeping in tents in the grounds and meeting in the ballroom for daily discussion and evening festivity. On Sundays this room was used for religious services of the mission type Cynicus preferred. Young art students often stayed at the castle. Workers' organisations came on bicycles and in buses. The employees of Guardbridge papermill and people from all over the East of Scotland flocked to concerts and dances and whist-drives. Cynicus sang comic songs in his weak old cracked voice, led them in choruses, played organ, piano and harp. He and Annie welcomed children. Though Annie loved them she could not conquer her native reserve and only watched as her brother regaled them with songs and stories. The local people almost looked on the castle as their social club, and on the Andersons, shabby though they were, as the first in the parish.

The visitors book, preserved from 1912 till a month after Cynicus's death, records their variety. They came from Dundee and Fife, Perthshire, industrial Lanarkshire and Ayrshire, Edinburgh, London and the USA; during the Great War soldiers from Cumberland and Canada received hospitality, and after it airmen, St Andrews university students, church choirs, nuns and ILP cycling clubs. Most were simple people and children, yet some had the tact to quote Cynicus verses as their motto. Just a few days before his death a party of forty came from Dundee for a dance, equipped with a professional exhibition dance couple. 'Mr Anderson took great delight in singing the many verses of "Kate Dalrymple", his party piece, at the interval.'

The dances were a constant source of friction between the Andersons and their nearest neighbour, Mr Menzies, but busloads of colliery workers or crowds of young folk from neighbouring towns raised a little cash and kept brother and sister alive. Their neighbour saw the many visitors only as unpleasant disturbance in a rural backwater. He complained to the police on one occasion that revellers threw stones through his greenhouse. Cynicus sent the police a venomous letter:

20th May 1930

Dear Sir

I had a visit from Mr Hepburn this evening anent the complaint made to you by my neighbour Mr John Menzies about the Dance held at the Castle last Friday. It is now nearly 30 years since I built Castle Cynicus purposely to be devoted to the public service for Picnics, Religious Services, Dances and Entertainments of every kind. Being bequeathed to the public and trustees having been appointed, I protest in the public interest against any unwarranted interference by Mr Menzies. This gentleman with a full knowledge of the facts came and erected a bungalow within a hundred yards of my residence and ever since has taken exception to every entertainment at the castle, Religious Services included. As a neighbour and a gentleman he could easily have called my attention to any supposed irregularity instead of calling in the Police but he hasn't even spoken to me for years and conducts himself with such ostentatious vulgarity as to be the laughing stock of the district. Knowing his antecedents as I do I naturally resent his interference.

The dance will take place on Friday as advertised and it is for you in the public interest to see that everything is properly conducted.

Yours faithfully

Martin Anderson

P.S. I am keeping a copy of this for reference if required.

Menzies was unable to stop the dances, but eventually he had the last word.

A PARTING TEAR.

Chapter 18—The End of a Dream 1931–39

WHAT GAVE CYNICUS the strength to fight on? Shabby and emaciated, spending his old age in the cold, unfinished castle, beset with daily difficulties of all descriptions, aware that his art was forgotten, he was nevertheless unbowed. The answer is to be found in *Through Wisdom's Glasses,* in particular in an essay which dealt with genius. Recycling as ever, he used it verbatim for a Burns' Night address he gave in Glasgow in 1931. If he applied it more or less to Burns, he applied it even more to himself.

> 'Genius' said Wisdom, 'is a chance product, and Nature seems very impartial as to where or on whom she confers it. Adversity seems its natural soil, and like the wall flower it thrives best among ruins and waste places… When Nature has no particular use for a man, she sends him floating down to oblivion on a competence. It is only her favourites, those for whom she has some purpose, she casts on the waters of affliction in the great ocean of Life.'

The conviction that his art was for all time was what gave him strength, so he could disregard the temporary neglect of his pictures. There are hints that he felt he had a special destiny. It may be ridiculous for a humorous cartoonist to claim genius, but there is no denying that in his cartoons he caught human archetypes.

Cynicus's death fell on his seventy-eighth birthday. A Mr Adamson held regular dancing classes in the studio ballroom. On 14th April 1932

he and Cynicus were having a chat before the children's class arrived, when Cynicus suddenly collapsed and died.

Cynicus was laid to rest in the Martin family grave in Tayport Old Churchyard. Pallbearers included his godson Martin Anderson Graham, the retired Edinburgh policeman Mr Paterson, and the Misses Peden, daughters of an old Dundee friend. The funeral was never paid for, and there is to this day no inscription on the stone.

Obituaries appeared in most papers, both local and national. The *Times* printed a number of inaccuracies, such as that he published a volume of memoirs and collected the museum curios on his wide travels. It was an habitué of the studio, someone who knew a fact never mentioned by any other writer—that the Drury Lane shop stood next to an old cemetery—who wrote an anonymous obituary of 'the Scottish adventurer', condemning the 'gushing notice which appeared in the *St James's Gazette*', the rush 'for examples of his vulgar drawings', and condescendingly concluded '" Cynicus" had a certain uncouth talent'. Something still rankled after more than thirty years.

Tiny Miss Annie Anderson was left alone with Miss Duncan in the crumbling mansion for ten months more. After Christmas William in Southend died of a heart attack like his brother, so she was the last

SPIRITUAL CONSOLATION.

survivor of that intimate group of siblings. In her long life she had quietly displayed the same tenacity as her famous brother. She too had refused to submit to defeat. Trained as an artist and a teacher, when required she had developed a fine organising talent, whether superintending the child colourists, catering for excursionists at the castle, or keeping the peace (mostly) between her brothers and sisters. And she had to manage Martin's occasional fits of resentment, obstinacy and depression.

A visitor to the castle related an extraordinary anecdote. The rope holding the flag on top of the forty-five foot tower had broken. Miss Annie in her long skirt mounted the parapet and jumped up until she caught it. Only the spectator blanched at the risk she so blithely took. Annie was 83 when she died at the castle in February 1933, the very last of the Andersons of Tayport.

No will was confirmed for either Martin or Annie. There was nothing to leave. Martin's old legacy to Bob Graham's widow of a pound a week for life was just a memory. But there were unpaid taxes still outstanding, and the Fife sheriff was called on to authorise the futile expedient of a warrant sale. More than a year after Annie's death the dust sheets were removed, and crowds tramped through the cold, damp rooms. A warrant sale does not expect to realise good prices: it is a punishment, a humiliation. Luckily, the Andersons were past caring.

The library and the museum were not touched. The ballroom offered good pickings. The baby grand piano was sold for ten shillings to a club in St Andrews, where it continued to entertain. The harp remained unsold, as did the famous pictures of Sunrise and Sunset inset in the walls. The French clock and its matching ornaments from the mantelpiece realised thirty shillings. A plaster bust of Cynicus as a youth was knocked down for four shillings. A volume of political pamphlets dated 1820—a valuable rarity—went for two shillings; his butterfly collection three shillings; 'old coins' five shillings; two near lifesize bronze statues eight shillings, the same price as a coal scuttle. The Fifers were interested in more practical items—his sundial and a garden bench. Amid hilarity women outbid each other for his exotic walking sticks. But the crowd of three hundred was disappointed, for as soon as the sheriff officer had made enough to clear the arrears of rates and expenses he closed the sale.

A local reporter, shown round the museum by an old friend of Cynicus, wrote:

The museum founded by "Cynicus" in the tower above remained locked up, musty and rather dilapidated. None of its hundreds of curios was sold. It seemed to brood over the noisy spectacle below, a memorial to the whim of a famous man. When I climbed into the tower and entered the museum a bat flew from behind a case… There are rows of cases of coins, some of which are very old, and of ivories and semi-precious stones used for decorative purposes. The shade of "Cynicus" was probably glad that his "den" in the tower was left untouched.

Instead, his valuable collections remained to be vandalised or stolen years later.

The Lockerby Almshouse Charity was the real owner of Castle Cynicus, under the administration of the Andersons' solicitor Marchbank. But by then he was dead, leaving trustees to take final possession of the Andersons' Tayport properties and tussle with the County Assessor or the Inland Revenue over the rates or taxes due on the castle. The multipicity of bonds over the property must have caused difficulty. Then there was the Castle Cynicus Scheme of 1921, though that was perhaps dead and forgotten.

Meanwhile the unkempt grounds became a picnic spot, while the house was left to rot. For four years it stood quietly mouldering. Heavy slates broke their pegs and slipped askew; rain poured in.

Local children made up stories about a haunted house, dared each other to go up the avenue in the dark. Eventually the inevitable occurred. Someone threw the first stone through a window. When nothing happened others followed. Pigeons moved in. Thereafter picnickers felt free to look round the open house and remove any item they fancied. By word of mouth the rumour spread. Albums of prints and cartoons, and *objets de vertu* from the museum found new homes. Since very few people at that time had cars, the larger objects remained where they were until the vandals arrived. Then the Inca mummy was dismembered, stuffed birds were torn apart, the Greek vases smashed, the statues beheaded, the Sunset painting slashed, the floors littered ankle deep with torn-up books.

Ironically, Cynicus had wanted his house to be open to the public after his death.

And still the Lockerby Almshouse Charity did nothing to safeguard its property. In the words of a local resident, 'The place has been practically wrecked. I don't think there's a whole window left, or even a door, and pigeons are nesting in the rooms.' A local newspaper described the wreckage, and unwittingly encouraged more acquisitive visitors to walk up from Leuchars Junction. Menzies in the neighbouring house now had indeed something to complain of.

At last, in April 1938, six years to the day after Cynicus died, his castle and grounds were offered for sale. The castle that had cost £3,000 was offered at £100. Despite newspaper publicity there were no bids. The Charity went to sleep again. The castle deteriorated further. An airman from Leuchars, cycling past, admired the building and asked himself why such a beautiful house was being allowed to go to wreck and ruin. Finding the doors open, he went in, and picked up from the filthy littered floor a copy of the *Fatal Smile*.

The castle was re-offered in January 1939—castle, conservatory, stabling, gardens and twelve and a half acres of land, for £250. This time there was interest. The one man who was determined to get possession was Menzies. He got the lot for £370. Not a penny of that sum was left over to repay the Lockerby Almshouse Charity which had lent £750.

Asked what he proposed to do with the castle and grounds, Menzies

replied, 'I cannot tell you. You will see within a day or two.' A rumour got about that the new proprietor might close the avenue that had been Cynicus's last major enterprise. For years it 'has been available for the use of the villagers, and has been a favourite walk. It runs for about a quarter of a mile up the side of the grounds, connecting a lane at the foot with the quarry road at the top. Though in no sense a right-of-way, its use has been a valued privilege,' commented the *Evening Telegraph,* and asked the purchaser whether he intended to close it. 'Well, I don't know. I suppose I may.'

The next week a notice 'Strictly Private' appeared at the foot of the avenue, and work began on demolishing the castle. It had been built to last. The ashlar work was sold for re-use, the felsite returned to the quarry from which it had come thirty-seven years before, to be ground down for road metal. The lintel of 'Truth the lyre' ended up somewhere in Angus. A year later a former guest at the castle braved the 'Strictly Private' notice to view the site of previous delights, and found 'everything very changed'. The cottage where she had holidayed was rebuilt, but Castle Cynicus was gone. So too was Menzies. He died in August 1939.

The name 'Cynicus Castle' was erased from the Ordnance Survey map. Cynicus was all but forgotten. Another war passed over the land, another generation arose. Yet he is not quite forgotten. Partly it is nostalgia for a world never known, partly fascination with his personality, partly interest in his art. Postcard collectors mention his cards with respect and Labour historians esteem the political cartoons. Others collect his books, though they appeared in such limited editions that they are hard to find. Should one turn up in the auction room it is eagerly bid for.

His Work

His work still stands out as unique. Like the albums of the 1890s the postcards amuse with fun and puns, social criticism and black humour. They make the reader laugh and wince, and laugh again. Of course his humour was of its time when it poked fun at ugliness, old spinsters and drunks. But mostly his designs caricature eternal human frailties. He was a master at portraying ordinary people's failings—their folly and self-importance, weakness and greed, their discreditable emotions lurking beneath self-righteousness, their hypocrisy masquerading as respectability. Sometimes kindly, sometimes caustic, he presents the laughable in human nature. We recognise the faces, the gestures, the postures, because they are so well observed.

If some of his jokes now seem dated, many of his serious cartoons are still topical. We recognise the archetypes in the portrait gallery of a corrupt Establishment: Capitalism grown powerful by exploiting labour; an established Church staffed by worldly sluggards; the Law intent on fat fees; Journalism fishing in a cesspool of gossip; not to forget the Monarchy given up to ignoble pleasures. A century later the themes are still with us.

He started out ahead of his time. When he published the *Satires of Cynicus* the social ideas it embodied were of intense interest. He went on to pour out what seemed at first an inexhaustible flood of invention. But actually he spent the rest of his career reworking the first achievement, recycling original ideas until they became old-fashioned. From first to last the style of humour did not change. Without the support of his whole family was he unable to develop? Or after the failure of *Cartoons Social and Political* was he afraid to develop?

His Character

Let us try to sum up the character of Martin Anderson. On the one hand, an attractive social personality predisposed people in his favour. On the other hand, he could put people's backs up. In Glasgow, in Dundee, in London, in Edinburgh, in Fife, it took him no time to collect a band of faithful friends. He was eminently clubbable, in fact he founded clubs, but some friends turned into enemies.

In 1891 he delighted London with the freshness of youth. The boyish impression created by his small, slight figure and enthusiastic talk entranced Bohemia. Partly it came naturally, partly he worked at it. Sometimes he offended, unable to resist a witty remark even when it might wound. Hence the venomous obituary, hence the malevolent newspaper comment on his success with postcards. Hence Peggy Webling's caricature of him in *Felix Christie*.

He retained all the egotism of youth, or genius, his life long. He accepted any sacrifice from the family as due to his talent: 'Loans from my sisters, which need not be repaid.' And the siblings seem to have accepted their role.

His perpetual youthfulness shows too in his capacity for shrugging off responsibility, his vehement likes and dislikes, his black and white view of society. For him the rich and powerful had no redeeming features. They must be hypocrites or scoundrels.

Yet he was not so much an innocent as an actor. From early days he presented the public with an edited version of Martin Anderson, making himself out to be younger than he was, using his good looks to advance himself.

He manipulated the media throughout. His memoirs were cunningly contrived. Between vagueness and boasting he conveniently omitted some events and slanted others. He refused to copy a painting he had sold as a one-off, but forgot he republished a second thousand *Satires of Cynicus*. He said he abandoned London when London abandoned him.

He could be spiteful. He took out on William and Nelly his resentment at London's change of heart. He could be stubborn, refusing to repay a loan although at the time he had money to build himself a castle. In later life he developed an irascibility that fed on his sense of genius unrecognised.

But after all, he overcame trials that would have soured most men and reverses of fortune that would have reduced most to despair. Against all the evidence, he retained his belief that 'The best is now, the best is yet to be.' Instead of complaining, he filled the ballroom with students and dancers. In a snobbish age he met all classes on an equal footing. If he sometimes had reservations about the prudence of the

THE WAY OF THE WORLD.

working man on strike, he did his best for those whom the Depression had cast into unemployment. He was generous—with his money when he had any, with his time and thought when he had none.

When all the negative aspects of his character have been told over, a chorus of appreciation weighs down the balance on the other side: 'He thought about others before thinking about himself... kept his childlike heart... a kindlier soul never existed... his instinct was to make others happy. To anyone in need he would have handed over his last penny... At heart he was a Socialist... farflung benevolence, an ever genial enthusiasm for sharing his possessions... a kindly man with a tremendous sense of fun...a modest unpretentious man.' All these encomiums cannot be wrong. His social conscience was no pose.

Alas, " It is not always *May*,"

'Tis very often *Must*.

NOTES

Unless otherwise stated, quotations are from Cynicus's memoirs published in twelve instalments in the *Glasgow Evening News* between 24 February and 11 March 1930.

CHAPTER 1—A Rural Childhood 1854–68

* 'their successful ancestors'—from his memoirs: 'Our uncle, John Connon, was a barrister in London, and became an Indian judge, and ultimately became Chief Magistrate of Bombay, owned and edited the Bombay Gazette, and founded the Connon School. Another uncle, George Gardener, was a poet, published in Cupar Gardener's [Gardiner's] Miscellany. My grandfather, William Anderson, and our grand-uncles, James and Thomas Neish, introduced the jute industry into Dundee.' Nellie Mitchell, who became Madame Melba the singer, was another relative.

* Mrs Oliphant (1828-97) set her novel *The Primrose Path* in North East Fife.

* 'The Portuguese baron'—Emmanuel Suarez, butler at Earlshall.

* J A Hammerton: *Humorists of the Pencil* (London 1905), p.101.

* Rosebank Place—Census 1871 Cambuslang, Book I.

CHAPTER 2—An Urban Adolescence 1868–77

* 'a minute notebook'—in the authors' possession, along with the fabric designs. The Eastfield pit accident was reported in *Hamilton Advertiser* on 15 November 1873.

* 'Weir'—young Martin was a favourite with the Weir boys' mother, a granddaughter of Robert Burns who imparted to him folk tales and the tenets of the Plymouth Brethren. The brothers, then marine engineers, later founded the company now known as the Weir group. The future Lord Weir attended Mrs Anderson's dame school.

* St Mungo Art Club, instituted 1874, aims given in *Glasgow PO Directory* 1877-78, p.130.

* On Cynicus's death certificate his father is designated 'flax merchant'. The son seems to have visited him in Leuchars, for a sketch of Earlshall dovecot is dated 1871, during the Cambuslang years.

* For *News of the Week* he first illustrated 'The Jesuits' Prey' and other serial stories (10 February–22 December 1877). Wickes also owned the *Glasgow News* and *Glasgow Evening News*.

CHAPTER 3—To London 1878–79

* William Sanderson, see *Edinburgh Directory* 1877 and 1881 census of Edinburgh 692/2/22. His friends, Cynicus recalled, were 'big, bluff hearty men who came to life marvellously once the port had begun to circulate'.

* 'The Music Lesson' in RSA Catalogue of Exhibitors 1878, no.6. Also no.285, 'Wild Flowers' in 1880.

* 'the foot passenger of a morning'—*Globe*, 16 November 1894, front page, referring back 'a dozen years'.

* 'an extremely well-to-do patron'—Cynicus gives name and address as Netlam Giles, The Terrace, Richmond. A different version of what seems the

same story is recounted by J A M Muir in 'Cynicus, An Artist Enigma', *Scots Magazine*, May 1958, in which Cynicus enjoys 'a marvellous dinner' in the West End.

* Karl E Maison: *Daumier Drawings* (New York 1960). The Daumier retrospective exhibition at the Durand-Ruel gallery ran from April to June 1878 to coincide with the Paris 'World's Fair'.

* Cynicus's 'Futurity' resembles Daumier's 'Epouvantée de l'Héritage'.

CHAPTER 4—By Our Staff Artist 1880–85

* 'John Leng'—A H Millar: *The Dundee Advertiser 1801-1901: A Centenary Memoir* (Dundee 1901), p.46f.

* *Dundee PO Directory* 1882-86—William produce broker, Martin artist, at Hillgrove, Hill Street, Broughty Ferry (upper part of Herschel House).

* 'Dundee had jute mills'—Billy Kay, ed.: *The Dundee Book, an Anthology of Living in the City* (Edinburgh 1990).

* 'Brown family gravestones'—*Dundee Advertiser* 10 March 1884, p.7. Signed drawings are rare, but he uses his MA monogram in the series 'The Castles and Mansions of Fife and Kinross' in *People's Journal*, e.g. Crawford Priory (29 May 1886) and Earlshall (31 July 1886).

* 'serials'—e.g. *Job's Reflections; Recollections of a London Detective*.

* 'booklets'—e.g. *Rosetty Ends or The Chronicles of a Country Cobbler; Readings Pithy and Pawky; Black Kalendar of Scotland*.

* A S Boyd: *Glasgow Men and Women* (London 1905), describes *Quiz* in introduction. Both he and Anderson later worked on the *Idler*.

* 'For unmitigated squalor'—*Quiz* 16 May 1884, p.92.

* 'great frilled caps'—the mutch so favoured by Martin Anderson was already out of date and is one reason that contemporaries often termed his cartoons 'quaint'.

* 'Amor Vincit Omnes'—*Quiz* 6 April 1883.

CHAPTER 5—Getting Into His Stride 1886–90

* 'a friend later wrote'—'Norval' Scrimgeour, in Cynicus's obituary, *People's Journal*, 16 April 1932.

* The de luxe edition of the *Satires* was to be printed on superfine plate paper for subscribers only, at 6/6. The de luxe edition of the *Humours* would be offered on handmade paper, uncut and bound in buckram, numbered, retouched and signed by Cynicus, at three guineas.

* We do not know exactly when he resigned from Leng's employment. He says he was 'eight years in Dundee'. The 'late eighties' are repeatedly mentioned as the time he went to London, e.g. in obituaries.

CHAPTER 6—The Great Adventure 1890–91

* 'an erstwhile friend'—Peggy Webling: *Peggy, The Story of One Score Years and Ten* (London 1924), p.192.

* *Pall Mall Budget* 12 March 1891, pp.14-15, mentioned the price of 1 guinea, while in the same month the *Review of Reviews* after a warm review gave the old price of 10/6.

* *Ariel* published 'The Modern Use of a Peer', *scil.* as a lure to investors,

speculators placed his name at the head of the company prospectus. 'Time's Rubbish Shoot' disposes of Law, Church, peerage and party politics, society verse, Impressionism and Theosophy. These were re-used in *Cartoons Social and Political*.

* 'scarcely the way to set the Thames on fire'—Hammerton, p.100.

* 'Cynicus made a good host'—*Peggy*, p. 192.

* Pauline Johnson came to England to promote her book of poems *The White Wampum*.

* For Frances Hodgson Burnett, see Ann Thwaite: *Waiting for the Party* (London 1974).

* 'Norval' Scrimgeour in *People's Journal* 16 April 1932.

* Sir William Allan (1837-1903), engineer and Liberal MP, wrote books of patriotic verse and presented them to his friends: *Dictionary of National Biography*. The authors have a letter of 9 July 1894, sent to 'Dear Sinnikus' with his poems.

* D Marquand: *Ramsay MacDonald* (London 1977).

* J K Jerome (1859-1927): *My Life and Times* (2nd ed. London 1983), p. 137. 'A Scotchman who signed himself "Cynicus" drew cartoons for *The Idler*: clever sketches, with a biting satire. He had a quaint studio in Drury Lane; and lived there with his sisters [*sic*]. One used to meet Ramsay MacDonald there. He was a pleasant, handsome young man.'

* Caroline Benn: *Keir Hardie* (London 1992).

* K O Morgan: *Keir Hardie Radical and Socialist* (London 1975).

CHAPTER 7—A Vagabond 1891–92

* *Scotsman*—14 September 1891, p.3.

* *Globe*—23 September 1891, p.6. The reviewer declared: 'The two books of his achievement that have been issued from Drury Lane each contain something under 200 drawings, no small record for less than a couple of years work.'

* Henry Anketell was the son of W R Anketell, himself a campaigner against absentee landlords in Ireland with pamphlets published 1843-44. (The *15th Report of the Land Nationalisation Society* 1895-96 mentions that the campaign van with Henry Aldridge as lecturer visited Tayport.)

* T R Threlfall was instrumental in founding the Labour Electoral Association in 1887.

* 'Another political caravanner'—*Pall Mall Budget* 26 May 1892, p.764.

* Douglas Sladen: *Twenty Years of My Life* (London 1915), p.162, '[Cynicus] won himself undying popularity here by bringing to one of those teas a charmingly pretty young American—Alice Livingston.' It was at the socialite Sladen's house that Cynicus first met Marie Corelli and Phil May. May's biographer, James Thorpe, noted in *Phil May: Master-draughtsman and Humorist 1864-1903* (London 1932) p.74, that 'Several of these [*Sydney*] *Bulletin* drawings, in their broad, aggressive humour and somewhat crude drawing, hint that May was not above accepting a suggestion from the work of "Cynicus".' Thorpe lists five cartoons in particular. May espoused the 'leaving-out method'; Cynicus believed in outline and 'brevity'.

167

* History of Vagabond Club—*Echo* 4 January 1893, front page.
* 'To bring editors and contributors together'—G B Burgin in *Sketch* 29 August 1894.

CHAPTER 8—Reacting to Criticism 1892–94

* 'One came across them'—*Peggy*, p.192.
* P Webling: *Felix Christie* (London 1912), p.220 and p. 46; also in *The Story of Virginia Perfect* (London 1909) p.211 'They're apt to be vulgar. They're not the sort of thing to hang in one's drawing-room. As a man told me the other day—of course it was one of my best friends—all I do is to glorify the gutter.'
* *Review of Reviews* reviewed the *Fatal Smile* in February 1893.
* Sir William Craigie (1867-1957): letters in St Andrew University Library.
* *Globe* 16 November 1894, front page, 'The Downfall of Drury-Lane'.

CHAPTER 9—Debacle 1894–98

* 'he sold ten cartoon originals'—information from Wellgate Library, Dundee. In the *Daily Graphic* 17 September 1894: 'All artists—save the disciples of black and white—are complaining of the the times and the difficulty of selling pictures.'
* 'purchasing the Tayport house'—Fife Sasines 31 March 1894, no.406.
* Peter Keary (1865-1915), part-owner and editor of *Pearson's Weekly*, journalist and author of best-selling *Secrets of Success*, *Do It Now*, and *Get On or Get Out*.
* 'Drooko' Wright's advertisement 'A Breezy Day' appeared in the *Bailie* 5 September 1894.
* June 1895 cartoon republished in booklet by J Timewell: *The State Carriage* (1895).
* *Weekly Times & Echo*—the commission lasted from 23 June to 3 November 1895 (also re-using old material).
* 'the *Idler* accepted a short article'—in *Idler* May 1896, p.631f. Mary Anderson was an American actress, who married, retired from the stage and became hostess to literary and journalistic figures such as J M Barrie (see Janet Dunbar: *J M Barrie: The Man Behind The Image* (London 1970).)
* 'Cynicus was the most sincere admirer'—*Peggy*, p.192; cf. *Felix Christie*, p.46.
* '"Cynicus" was the soul of good-nature'—Burgin: *More Memoirs*, p. 74f.
* James Greig (1861-1941): letter to *Glasgow Evening News* 7 March 1930.
* 'It was advice in keeping'—*Peggy*, p.194.
* Mrs Keary's letter: *Glasgow Evening News* 26 March 1930.
* 24 Brunswick Street—Electoral Register London, Strand, Long Acre Ward, 1897-99.

CHAPTER 10—Starting Again 1898–1902

* 'it was viable'—in 1898 he had to mortgage The Grove for £400.
* 'a London firm'—Cynicus's memoirs.
* Mrs Susan Reid, aged 90, described her experience as a colourist in 1974 in

the *Evening Telegraph*. In conversation with Wilfrid Grubb she recalled there were 6 other girl colourists in 1896, they worked in an upstairs studio across the road from The Grove, and occasionally Cynicus came in to give them sweets or once an insect each.

* *Daily Graphic* 29 August 1894: 'On Saturday next 1st September the public will have the privilege of sending through the inland post as postcards private cards bearing ½d adhesive stamp.' The permitted measurements are shown. Court cards, the official Post Office size, were smaller and squarer than later postcards.

* 'Messrs Blum & Degen'—in his memoirs Cynicus does not mention this firm. Instead he writes he had a visit from 'old Mr Harrap of the well-known firm of publishers, who made me an offer of six guineas each for six sketches for postcards. They sold at fivepence for the packet of six and met with enormous success.' A Blum & Degen advertisement of November 1900 mentions three Cynicus sets for sale.

* Postcards which provide the beginnings of a sentence for the sender to complete are termed write-aways. Blum & Degen's Cynicus cards are thought to be both the first write-aways and the first comic postcards (see *Picture Postcard Annual* 1983, pp.8, 95).

* Letter to *Courier and Advertiser* 31 March 1969 from D Wilkie Gahan of Broughty Ferry; his father drew a pencil portrait of Cynicus in 1931.

* Letter to *Scots Magazine* August 1958, p.407, from Frank Willsher of Philadelphia.

* 'Keir Hardie had come'—David Lowe: *From Pit to Parliament* (London 1923), p.175.

* Nelly and Loxton Hunter married in the district of Eltham, Kent, with William as witness.

* *Sunday Mail* 5 January 1930, p.7.

* *Dundee Directory* 1891 listed churches. From Cynicus's script for a Burns' Night address in 1931: 'Being now well over the "Three-score and ten" let me recall to you the Scotland of my early days, the quiet village life in the country towns; the clear-cut line that divided the Rich from the Poor, "Those who had and those who hadn't"; the narrow-minded rivalry between the Churches, as many as five and six distinct sects in one small country town, having little or no fellowship with each other.'

* *Dundee Advertiser* 2 November 1901, p.8; *Courier* 2 November 1901, p.5.

CHAPTER 11—The Company and The Castle 1902–04

* The Cynicus Publishing Company had employed John's father, James Allan, as a part-time commercial traveller. John was known as Allan Junior.

* Dissolved Companies File No.5034, Scottish Record Office.

* 'submitted plans for premises'—Tayport Burgh Commissioners Minutes.

* 'three-colour printing process'—full description in *Postcard Connoisseur* March 1904, p.9. It featured CPCo Ltd in this, its first issue and gave away a complimentary Cynicus card. It considered 'this somewhat erratic genius' to be 'unique'.

* F Alderson: *The Comic Postcard in English Life* (Newton Abbot 1970); Anthony Byatt: *Picture Postcards and Their Publishers* (Malvern 1978).

* G T Webber: 'The Rise and Fall of the Edwardian Picture Postcard Boom' in *Picture Postcard Monthly* (Nottingham) June, July, September, October 1990 and March 1994.

* 'made postmen agitate for higher wages'—*People's Friend* 2 November 1903, p.885.

* 'he bought thirteen acres'—Fife Sasines 5 September 1902, no.1770.

* *People's Journal* 20 December 1902, p.8: two sketches show how the completed house (with balcony) and printing works in Tayport will look. Full description of the house in *Fife News* 20 December 1902, p.2.

* 'He promptly bonded it' —Fife Sasines 5 August 1903, no.1605.

* 'In March 1905'—hand-bill advertising the concert in authors' possession.

* 'in 1904 Bob and family moved'—information from Bob's granddaughter Mrs Effie Ramsay, Leuchars, and from Cynicus's farewell letter to Bob, dated 28 September 1904, in authors' possession.

CHAPTER 12—The Postcard Craze 1904–07

* 'four hundred and twenty million picture postcards'—from A J Butland and E A Westwood: *Picture Postcards and all about them* (Teddington 1959), p.10.

* *Picture Postcard and Collectors' Chronicle* February and April 1903.

* 'it could offer the trade'—*PPCC* May 1905. *PPCC* made frequent reference to CPCo Ltd.

* 'novelty cards'—others included real tartan under transparent paper, an imitation 'Wedding Ring', the 'Matched Heart' (a red heart pierced by an imitation match), artificial flowers 'gummed on or under transparent gelatine', a miniature doll attached to ribbon. Also real substances, e.g. coal, granite, jute, a piece of tow ('A lock of hair I send to you, Although 'tis false, my heart is true'), a piece of sponge ('I'm a bit of a sponge as well'), tobacco ('Put this in your pipe and smoke it!'), cork ('To keep you afloat') from *PPCC* passim.

* James Douglas RSW (1858-1911)—obituary in *Dundee Advertiser* 24 July 1911.

* 'Jotter' was Walter Hayward Young (1868-1920); Charles Gustave Louis Phillips (1863-1944).

* 'pirated by Tacon & Co'—Byatt, p.280: 'In 1908, Cynicus was awarded £12 damages.'

CHAPTER 13—Boom and Bust 1907–11

* '"Hullo! What's making your hair stand on end?"' —*Weekly Welcome* 4 December 1907, p. 1457.

* Sir James Caw: *Scottish Painting Past and Present 1620-1908* (Edinburgh 1908), p. 468. Similarly, James H Thorpe: *English Illustrators of the Nineties* (London 1935) p.153—'"Cynicus"...produced satirical cartoons—somewhat crude in drawing but popular in their direct appeal...They were to be seen in most of the print-sellers' windows.'

* 'In the 1908-09 depression'—G D H Cole: *British Working Class Politics 1832-1914* (London 1941), pp. 194, 196, 198.

* David Graham's diary is held by North East Fife District Museum Service. His entry for 24 April 1910 states a debt of £1,600 has just come to light. He mentions frequent visits by Mr Walsh from Glasgow, e.g. to have ban-

ners painted. In *Forward* 15 October 1910 P Walsh advertises Cynicus pictures and cards, including 'The State Carriage'. 'The Pharisee's Prayer' from the *Satires* appeared in *Forward* on 14 May apropos of Leadhills strike.

CHAPTER 14—Disasters 1911–14

* Much of the casual information was provided by the late Ralph Fyfe-Smith, son of Cynicus's friend Jim Smith, in correspondence with Wilfrid Grubb.
* Cynicus's diary is held by North East Fife District Museum Service.
* *The Great Bank Fraud* (Edinburgh 1916), (2nd ed. Balmullo 1926).
* The CPCo Ltd was finally wound up on 9 June 1916.
* 'I should like to make it clear'—*People's Journal* 4 January 1930, p.17.
* 'We have never spoken'—*Sunday Express* 29 December 1929, p.3.
* John Anderson's mysterious death was reported in the *Courier* and the *Dundee Advertiser* on Monday, 7 October 1912. The two reports are full of contradictions. Cynicus makes no mention of the death in his memoirs, yet tells of Old Davies, an antiquarian bookseller in London: 'I went round to call on him one morning, but could get no response at the door. With the help, however, of the shopman next door, we forced our way in, and found the old man lying in the middle of his shop...'
* 'Three-quarters of an acre'—Fife Sasines 13 November 1913, no.1822, and 12 December 1913, no.2052.
* Cynicus Art Publishing Company, Basinghall Buildings, 52 Basinghall Street in *Kelly's Directory* Leeds 1914. Leeds cards numbered C301 to C396, unnumbered 'reversible heads' and miscellaneous cards were listed by Brian Lund in *Picture Postcard Annual* 1983.

CHAPTER 15—'WAR!' and Peace 1915–21

* '"I am now sixty-one"'—J A M Muir: *Scots Magazine* May 1958, p.92.
* Personal reminiscences of PC Paterson's son Philip. The Paterson family fed the hungry artist.
* Albert Mackie in *Scottish Daily Express* 13 August 1958; includes reminiscences from other Athenians.
* The authors possess some surviving Anderson family letters, presented by the late Bob Allan of Cupar.
* William Marwick is commemorated by a collection of Socialist literature in the Mitchell Library, Glasgow.
* *Dundee Advertiser* 18 July 1921, p.4.

CHAPTER 16—A Knock-Out Blow 1921–28

* 'a series of lectures'—handbill in Philip Paterson's collection.
* Marshall Bell paid the electricity bill: 'with a great flourish he wrote me an I.O.U. for £2 10s., which concluded the transaction'. From Albert Mackie's article in the *Scottish Daily Express* 13 August 1958.
* Fire chief's report courtesy of Mr R Church-Michael of Lothian & Borders Fire Brigade Library.
* Edinburgh Valuation Rolls 1924-26.

* 'Wayland Smith' in *Daily Record & Mail* 25 April 1934.
* Cynicus's correspondence with Ramsay MacDonald in the Public Record Office, reference PRO 30/69/747 XC11170 and PRO 30/69/1007 XC11170.
* 'A letter from the company's "manager"' —W A Hutchison—is inserted into the National Library of Scotland's copy of *The Great Bank Fraud.*
* 'my Earthworks and my Book'—letter to the Stewart family of Edinburgh, 5 January 1928. Tom Stewart was an Athenian often at Castle Cynicus.
* 'solo performance'—*Glasgow Evening News* 19 February 1930, p.4.
* '"My egg's cracked"' —anecdote from J M Stewart, the daughter of Tom.

CHAPTER 17—Cynicus Rediscovered 1928–1930
* 'The journalist...on New Year's Eve'—published the interview in *Sunday Mail* 5 January 1930, p.7.
* R. Fyfe-Smith's recollections: 'The last time I saw Martin Anderson was sometime between 1928 and 1930. He was dressed, as often before, in a rather shabby knickerbocker suit and his hair was grey and slightly long, but his beard was small and neat. He was very slim and was riding an old-fashioned bicycle.' Similarly, an elderly farm labourer recalled: 'He was a wee man wi' a close croppit beard like the King, and he aye wore a black velvet jaiket, and he rode a bike that was siller a' owre like my watch here. He aye pit me in mind o' a monkey in a show.' Quotation taken from 'A Visit to Castle Cynicus' by John Tonge, broadcast by the Scottish Home Service, BBC, on 23 April 1957.
* 'The Premier's Fife Friend' in *Evening Telegraph* 27 September 1929. *Daily Record & Mail* 2 April 1929 : 'Duchesses were among his guests, who included also several early Socialists.'
* 'One result of the publicity'—*People's Journal* 4 January 1930, p.17.
* 'a tense greeting'—*Sunday Express* 5 January 1930, front page.
* '"It is most cruel"'—*Daily Record & Mail* 4 January 1930, p.5.
* 'William returned to Southend'—According to the *Southend Standard* 2 January 1930, he apparently told the reporter: 'My father was the last man in Dundee to wear a pigtail. One day, when he was asleep, one of his daughters cut it off with a pair of scissors and it never grew again.' Surely his grandfather? William died on 27 December 1932.
* 'International Song of Peace'—*Glasgow Evening News* 22 February 1930, p.4. 'He has also composed a setting for it and has offered the Premier to let him hear it sung by a choir at his first visit to Scotland.'
* 'What I Did at Sixteen' in *Daily Record & Mail* 22 March 1930, p.13.
* Bob, Robert Husband Graham, died 16 April 1930, aged 72.
* Castle Cynicus visitors book is held by North East Fife District Museum Service.
* '"Kate Dalrymple"' —Isobel Herd's letter to the *Courier and Advertiser* 26 May 1969.
* 'Mr Hepburn'—a friend from Guardbridge papermill, who bequeathed his collection of Cynicus materials to North East Fife District Museum Service.
* 'Menzies'—John Stewart Menzies of Magicwell, Balmullo, a Leith shipowner and coal exporter. Died aged 79 in August 1939, shortly after demolishing Castle Cynicus.

CHAPTER 18—The End of a Dream 1931–39

* 'Burns Night address'—Cynicus's own script. He comforted himself with the observation: 'He only shows his littleness Who measures Genius by success.'

* 'A Mr Adamson'—Isobel Herd's father, letter to *Courier and Advertiser* 26 May 1969.

* Description of Cynicus's funeral in the *Courier and Advertiser* 19 April 1932, p. 3, and in *Scotsman*.

* 'The rope holding the flag'—Archie Callender of Edinburgh in correspondence with Wilfrid Grubb.

* 'a warrant sale'—a poster in J MacGregor's collection advertises the sale on 25 April 1934 and lists items to be sold 'By Warrant of the Sheriff of Fifeshire'.

* '"Cynicus" Relics up for Auction—Low Prices at Fife Sale' in *Daily Record & Mail* 26 April 1934, p.7.

* 'an old friend of Cynicus'—Graham L Wright of Falkirk, 'a well-known tenor'. He had been the Anderson's guest over New Year 1927-28 and 1928-29.

* 'The museum founded by "Cynicus"'—*Courier and Advertiser* 26 April 1934, p.5. Sir Flinders Petrie, the Egyptologist, had donated items. So had Elma Stewart, whose cousin, Gordon Cumming, was a big game hunter. A photo on the back page of *Glasgow Evening News* 6 January 1930 shows Cynicus in his museum.

* 'the vandals arrived'—'Vandalism at a Fife Castle' 28 August 1937 and 'Vandals Wreck Cynicus Castle' 30 August 1937, p.5, *Courier and Advertiser*.

* In the memoirs: 'I live in Castle Cynicus, but it is my hope that when I am gone it will be open to one and all.'

* 'An airman from Leuchars'—Mr Roy of Shrewsbury in correspondence with Wilfrid Grubb.

* 'Asked what he proposed'—*Evening Telegraph* 3 March 1939.

* 'a former guest'—Winifred, Tom Stewart's daughter.

Where's my Ball?

not able for his Tee

Keep your eye on the Ball

LIMITED EDITION OF 200
FULL COLOUR REPRODUCTION
CYNICUS
Golf and Law Prints
of about 1898

mounted on ivory board
12" by 10" overall
(300 mm by 250 mm)

£19.95 each post free
or £54.95 per set of three

from Forest Lodge,
Dykehead,
By Kirriemuir
DD8 4QN

"Justice is satisfied"

Strangers yet

A Lawsuit

The Law's Delay
From *Cartoons Social & Political*
(1893)
"God help the poor duffer
He trusts in a straw
Who hopes to get justice
By going to law."

£19.95 post free

from Forest Lodge,
Dykehead,
By Kirriemuir
DD8 4QN